An Attitude of Thankfulness

Second book in the Series
Christian Devotions & Quick Studies

By Jim Davenport

Lulu Paperback Edition

Copyright © 2011-2014
InfoSys Solutions Associates, Inc.
All rights reserved.

ISBN 978-1-312-66941-3

For information please address:
Jim Davenport
InfoSys Solutions Associates, Inc.
6637 Burnt Hickory Drive
Hoschton, GA 30548

http://jimdavenport.me/
jamesldavenport@gmail.com

Jim's books are also available in Paperback and Hardback
Editions

Preview and Order Books by Jim Davenport
http://jimdavenport.me/jims-books/

Book Description

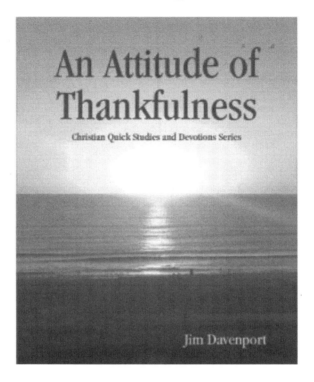

The twenty articles contained in this book cover topics close to Jim's heart including: thankfulness, thanklessness, the Christian's attitude, strength from God in the times of need, the sanctity of life and marriage, the consequences of our sin, praying with confidence, class warfare, and God's presence in our lives. One article recalls the Pine Lake Baptist Church fire and how God used that tragedy to further His purpose throughout the world from the small town of Stone Mountain, Georgia, USA.

This is the second in a series of books by Jim Davenport dealing with the general topic of *Christian Devotions and Quick Studies,* which was the title of the first volume.

Contents

... Dedication

This book is dedicated to my beloved wife and best friend Charlotte, who next to the Lord Jesus means more to me than anyone or anything else in this whole world!

Charlotte is patient, kind and loving no matter the situation. She allows me plenty of space to concentrate on my writing without even a hint of complaint. I know there are times that I neglect both her and my role as her husband, yet she never complains.

Charlotte faithfully reads all of my manuscripts and provides insightful and honest feedback. Without her I couldn't do much of anything. I love Charlotte with all of my heart and thank God every day for putting us together for life more than fifty years ago. Thank you God for the wonderful gift of Charlotte!

I also dedicate this book to our faithful son and daughter in law, Keven and Amy Davenport; our granddaughter Ashlyn, her husband Josh Murphy, and their two children Sawyer and Rhory; and to our grandson Mason Davenport ... each of whom I love with all my heart and thank God for each day!

... About Jim Davenport

Jim Davenport resides in the USA in Northeast Georgia, is a member of a Southern Baptist Church and is a retired Christian business man. Jim and his wife Charlotte have one son and daughter in law, Keven and Amy, two grandchildren – Ashlyn Davenport Murphy and husband Josh, and Mason Davenport. We have two great-grandchildren, Sawyer Joshua Murphy and Rhory Camille Murphy.

Jim and Charlotte own a mountain get-away home located on Lookout Mountain in Alabama where they spend many spring, summer and fall days working in their raised bed organic garden. Jim has served as a Deacon and Trustee in his local church most of his adult life and on the Executive Committee and Finance Committee of the Board of Trustees of Shorter University, an intentionally Christian institution located in Rome, Georgia.

Jim has a passion for the word of God and has always believed that Christian principles should guide every aspect of his life. He also loves Christian music and often served as a tenor soloist in his church. One of the highlights of his life was the nearly 20 years he spent singing with The Good News, a Southern Gospel quartet.

Jim served as an Information Technology professional his entire working career of 50 years holding senior positions in and consulting with hundreds of world-class organizations in the United States, Canada, Europe, Central and South America, Australia and New Zealand.

Jim remains as President and CEO of InfoSys Solutions Associates, Inc. and is a retired partner of IT Governance

Partners, LLC, both of which are "Trusted Advisor" technology and business consulting firms.

Jim has authored four books and is in the process of finishing a fifth. His blog is regularly read by readers from more than 120 countries.

Jim holds both a BS and an MS in Mathematics from Georgia State University in Atlanta, Georgia and completed Management Development Training at Emory University in Atlanta, Georgia.

… About My Blog – jimdavenport.me

jimdavenport

Biblically based Devotions & Quick Studies from a layman's perspective, gardening, interesting articles by others.

I am not an accomplished author by any stretch of the imagination. But I do enjoy writing about subjects that are important to me. I have spent much of my life in the information technology and consulting fields overseeing the successful preparation and presentation of tens of thousands of pages of complex technical and business documentation. At the same time, I have not written that much about what is really important to me … namely, sharing my Christian life experience with others in hopes that it would be meaningful to them in their Christian walk. Over the years as a Sunday School teacher at Pine Lake Baptist Church in Stone Mountain, Georgia, I put together hundreds of notes and outlines to guide my teaching. I always intended to develop some of those notes into a series of articles.

In late 2010 as my business career began to wind down and after suffering some health issues, I realized that I needed to move on with the development of the articles post haste. So I started a "blog" site using Wordpress.com to post articles as each was completed.

At times my posts are rather passionate and touch on subjects that are controversial. Admittedly, my posts are not very scholarly and are often quite opinionated. However, I always try to provide ample scripture to back up my points.

I realize that not everyone will appreciate my point of view, but my prayer is that I will make you think ... and in particular think about your relationship to our Lord and Savior, Jesus Christ. Your courteous comments are always welcome.

Please visit my blog site for additional articles and information about Jim Davenport.

An Attitude of Thankfulness

01 – An Attitude of Thankfulness

Background:

I was having trouble falling asleep recently and in my uncomfortable state a verse of scripture came to my mind like a bolt of lightning ... ***"O give thanks unto the Lord, for He is good; His mercy endureth forever."*** I lay there repeating the verse to myself several times. I was gradually convicted that all of my recent focus on the USA Presidential election had blinded me to what is **really** important in my life right now. I have so much for which to be thankful: my personal faith in the one and only triumvirate Almighty God, my wife, my children and grandchildren, and in May 2013 my great-grandchild, my extended family, my church, a happy life in a free country full of opportunity, my health, my material blessings, even my trials and temptations ... an endless list!

Rather than be elated or disappointed with the results of the election, I realized that my heart, mind and actions should be bathed with **An Attitude of Thankfulness** for Almighty God ... especially for His merciful, enduring, and steadfast love and protection for me and my family. I knew the verse was located in Psalms, but I could not remember which Psalm. So, I got out of bed and spent about thirty minutes finding and reading the scripture, Psalm 136 that had jolted me back to reality. Since I was wide awake by then, I decided to record some of my thoughts for later review and contemplation.

Since the Thanksgiving season is approaching I decided to expand on those thoughts and share them through this article trusting it will encourage you as much as it has me.

Scripture:

Psalm 136: 1-26 (KJV) – According to Wikipedia this Psalm is very important to the Jews. It is often called **"The Great Hallel"** and recited at the Passover meal after the **"The Lesser Hallel"** (Psalm 113-118). "It is punctuated by the refrain (*for His mercy endureth for ever*) that emphasizes God's loving-kindness is everlasting. There is mention in some references that this Psalm may also be used antiphonally (answering responsively) in Temple worship." For the purpose of this article let's break down Psalm 136 into three parts and look at it from the viewpoint of a Christian.

I. Verses 1-9: Be thankful and offer praise to **God as Creator** - As Creator God fashioned out of nothing the heavens and earth and stretched out His hand over the water and separated the dry lands from the water. He created the sun, the moon and the stars and all else in our Universe and beyond. Genesis 1:31 records *"And God saw every thing that he had made, and, behold, it was very good. And the evening and the morning were the sixth day."* God's creation is good … just as He is good. Lest we forget to be thankful and praise Him as Creator, the Psalmist reminds us in each verse of the Psalm that "**His mercy** (loving-kindness, love, charity) **endureth for ever.**" God will extend His mercy to all who seek Him. I am thankful to God and offer my Praise to Him as **Creator**.

*O give thanks unto the Lord; for **He is good**: for His mercy endureth for ever. O give thanks unto the **God of gods**: for His mercy endureth for ever. O give thanks to the **Lord of lords**: for His mercy endureth for ever. To Him who alone **doeth great wonders**: for His mercy endureth for ever. To Him that by wisdom **made the heavens**: for His mercy endureth for ever. To Him that **stretched out the earth above the waters**: for His mercy endureth for ever. To Him that **made great lights**: for His mercy endureth for ever: The **sun to rule by day**: for His mercy endureth for ever: The **moon and stars to rule by night**: for His mercy endureth for ever.*

II. Verses 10-22: Be thankful and offer praise to God as Israel's (and our) **God and Savior.** God demonstrated His mercy to us by delivering Israel from Egypt to the Promised Land. He was long-suffering and His mercy endured as Israel wavered back and forth in serving Him. God delivers us from the penalty of sin to redemption by accepting Jesus Christ to be our Savior. "**His mercy endureth for ever**" for all who accept Him. I am thankful to God and offer my Praise to Him because He is my **God and Savior.**

*To Him that **smote Egypt in their firstborn**: for His mercy endureth for ever: And **brought out Israel from among them**: for His mercy endureth for ever: With a **strong hand**, and with a **stretched out arm**: for His mercy endureth for ever. To Him which **divided the Red sea into parts**: for His mercy endureth for ever: And **made Israel to pass through** the midst of it: for His mercy endureth for ever: But **overthrew Pharaoh and his host** in the Red sea: for His mercy endureth for ever. To him which **led His people through the wilderness**: for His mercy endureth for ever. To Him which **smote great kings**: for His mercy endureth for ever: And **slew famous kings**: for His mercy endureth for ever: **Sihon king of the Amorites**: for His* *mercy endureth for ever: And **Og the king of Bashan**: for His mercy endureth for ever: And **gave their land for an heritage**: for His mercy endureth for ever: Even an heritage **unto Israel** his servant: for His mercy endureth for ever.*

III. Verses 23-26: *Be thankful and offer praise to God for **His blessings**. God is THE source for ALL of our blessings. He has delivered us from our enemies and Satan. He "**remembered us in our low estate**" of sin and blessed us with the coming and saving power of Jesus. He has put us in a position of stewardship over His possessions. He is THE provider for all of our needs giving us food, water, shelter, work, protection and everything else that is required. He owns it ALL and promises to provide for us both here on earth and for ever with Him in Heaven. I am thankful to God and offer my Praise to Him because of **His blessings**. Who **remembered us in our low estate**: for His mercy endureth for ever: And hath **redeemed us from our enemies**: for His mercy endureth for ever. Who **giveth food to all flesh**: for His mercy endureth for ever. **O give thanks unto the God of heaven**: for His mercy endureth for ever.*

Discussion:

Without a doubt the repetition of the phrase "*for his mercy endureth for ever*" by the writer (likely King David) of Psalm 136 was so thankful for God's **mercy** and the promise that it would **endure for ever**! What **An Attitude of Thankfulness**!

I learned in one of our Wednesday night Bible studies taught by my Pastor, Dr. Keith Pisani, more than three years ago that the Hebrew word translated as "mercy" in the English language versions of the Old Testament such as the King James Version (KJV) is "<u>chesed</u>" (חסד). Chesed is also translated as "loving-kindness," "love," and "compassion." In the New Testament translations, chesed is understood to be linked with the Greek word "agape," usually translated as "love" and "charity." The English Standard Version (ESV) of the Bible translates chesed as "steadfast love" in Psalm 136. The New International Version simply uses "love" to translate chesed. God's love for us endures for ever. I am still studying on this and will write an article later ... perhaps more than one.

I can't get any deeper than that on chesed as I am neither a Hebrew nor Greek scholar. For that matter, I am not an English scholar or a Bible scholar either. So let's settle on "mercy" as our translation for the purpose of this article.

Reflection:

Dean Doster

Reverend Dean Doster served as regional coordinator for Home Mission Board (now North American Mission Board) centered in Atlanta, Georgia for thirteen years during the 1980's and 1990's. Later Dean served as the Executive Director of the Louisiana Baptist Convention for eight years from 1998 – 2005. Previously Dean served as a regional coordinator for the Home Mission Board (now North American Mission Board) and as an associate executive director of the Tennessee Baptist Children's Home. He served as Pastor of several churches in Tennessee and Kentucky after being ordained to the ministry in 1973. He earned degrees from Bethel College in McKenzie, Tennessee, Southern Baptist Theological Seminary in Louisville, Kentucky, and Trinity Theological Seminary in Newburg, Indiana. Dean's degree was in expository preaching and there is no question that he is a soul winner and a great communicator both from the pulpit and one-on-one.

While serving as Interim Pastor at Pine Lake Baptist Church in Stone Mountain, Georgia, I was privileged to hear Dean preach an extended series of sermons on "attitude." That series had such an impact on my life. My wife will attest to that today as she questions my attitude by reminding me of Dean's teaching. Dean's personal attitude was such a tremendous asset to his ministry. He always had a smile and a word of encouragement. Dean helped me to realize that attitude is like an infectious disease. If you have a lousy or negative attitude all of the time, then those around you seem to catch the "virus" and also have lousy attitudes. If you have a thankful and joyful attitude, the same holds true. Christians have no reason to possess a negative attitude. After all, Jesus Christ paid the price for our sinfulness and we are guaranteed to spend an eternity with Him in Heaven. Christians should exhibit the attitude of a servant (a good topic for later). The life of Jesus provides us the model for the Christian's "servanthood."

As I grow older and reflect back on my life as a Christian, I can surely say that going about my daily life with in **An Attitude of Thankfulness** boosts my morale and better allows me to accomplish God's purpose for my life. It makes me happy and keeps me focused on the right things.

What about you? How is your attitude? Is it one of thankfulness? If not, will you change? God's "chesed" (loving-kindness, steadfast love, compassion) is Boundless Love!

Related Southern Gospel Music by The Good News:

- Boundless Love
- Listen to The Good News

02 – An Anchor in the Time of the Storm

Background:

The 2012 USA Presidential Election is now history and in an extremely close finish our president for the next four years will again be Barack Hussein Obama. Half of the USA population is ecstatic and the other half is tremendously disappointed. Legislative gridlock will continue as the Republicans retained control of the House and the Democrats still control the Senate.

Hurricane Sandy – Sunday October 25, 2012 begins its northern trek toward the USA NE coast.

Almost two weeks prior to the election, Hurricane Sandy made landfall in Jamaica on Wednesday, October 24, 2012. "The storm turned deadly in the Caribbean, and a hurricane/winter storm hybrid decimated regions along the U.S. East Coast" centered on New Jersey on October 29, 2012. Sandy has been described by many as the "storm of the century." Certainly it will be one of the ten costliest in the USA since 1900.

Robert Connolly, left, embraces his wife Laura as they survey the remains of the home owned by her parents that burned to the ground in the Breezy Point section of New York, Tuesday, Oct. 30, 2012. More than 50 homes were destroyed in the fire which swept through the oceanfront community during superstorm Sandy. At right is their son, Kyle. (AP Photo/Mark Lennihan)

The coverage for the Presidential election suddenly took a backseat to the continuous news reports of the significant destruction, power outages to more than 8.5 million homes and businesses, and the mounting death toll (74 in the USA and still rising as of November 3, 2012), particularly in New Jersey and New York, that resulted from Sandy. CNN and other networks chronicled the event both before and after the storm for days ('A loss for everybody': Communities start cleanup after Sandy).

Military rescues trapped victims in New Jersey

<u>Military and emergency response units</u> rescued people from homes and businesses isolated by the flooding. Major portions of New York city's subway system were crippled due to <u>flooding</u>. Mayor Bloomberg of New York City under pressure from all sides <u>cancelled the New York Marathon</u> as outrage mounted over using generators to power tents in Central Park that could power hundreds of homes still without power.

In the aftermath and recovery from the storm, there was an ongoing debate among USA and international news agencies that because of the storm's massive disruption on everyday life a significant number of voters would not able to reach the polls to cast their vote ... thus giving the edge to one candidate or the other. Most of the storm victims were still dealing with personal priorities that are currently more important than the election. What many were/are looking for is An *Anchor in the Time of the Storm.*

Scripture:

Hebrews 6:17-20 (ERV) – [17] *God wanted to prove that His promise was true. He wanted to prove this to those who would get what he promised. He wanted them to understand clearly that his purposes never change. So God said something would happen, and He proved what He said by adding an oath.* [18] *These two things cannot change: God cannot lie when He says something, and He cannot lie when He makes an oath. So these two things are a great help to us who have come to God for safety. They encourage us to hold on to the hope that is ours.* [19] **This hope is like an anchor for us. It is strong and sure and keeps us safe.** *It goes behind the curtain.* [20] *Jesus has already entered there and opened the way for us. He has become the high priest forever, just like Melchizedek.*

Discussion:

Hurricanes are not the only **storms** we will face in our lifetime. Life's **storms** take many forms including health issues, family problems, job loss, and job issues, financial trouble, divorce, death of a family member, anxiety, depression, doubt, fear, relationship issues, unjust rumors, chronic pain, etc. God Almighty knows that we will face such adversity throughout our lives. He knew the storms in our life would have the potential to sweep us away. So God provided a sure **anchor** for us in such times. That **anchor** is Jesus!

God's word, The Bible, is also an immovable **anchor** in the time of storms. In his sermon "Our Anchor in Times of Storm", <u>Dr. Charles Stanley</u> related ... "In the midst of hardship and pain, we can rely on the Bible for the stability, guidance, and security we need." Every word of The Bible is true and without error. As Dr. Stanley so aptly says, "The Bible **is the record of God's unfolding revelation of Himself** through the spoken Word, nature, history, and ultimately the coming of His Son Jesus Christ into the world."

In approximately 68 AD the writer of Hebrews, commonly attributed by most scholars as Paul ... but not conclusively, offered encouragement to those Christian Hebrew followers who were in the service of the Lord but in need of further spiritual maturity. Paul provided them the assurance that God would keep ALL of His promises by reminding them of the example of how Abraham received the promise of God through his faithfulness. In Hebrews 6: 13-15 Paul said *"[13] God made a promise to Abraham. And there is no one greater than God, so he made the promise with an oath in his own name—an oath that he would do what he promised. [14] He said, "I will surely bless you. I will give you many descendants."[c] [15] Abraham waited patiently for this to happen, and later he received what God promised."*

As Dr. Stanley pointed out in his sermon, sometimes we are responsible for our own storms. The sin in our lives is often the cause for a storm. At other times we show poor judgment in our decision-making bringing on a storm. Satan also causes adversity and storms in our life as he attempts to draw us away from God. Others, such as family and friends, can bring storms into our lives. At times even God brings storms into our life, but be assured that such storms are always for our own good. Sometimes it takes a storm to get our attention, purify us from sin, cause us to surrender to Him, and equip us to serve Him.

In closing his sermon, Dr. Stanley gives some scripture verses reminding us that God's Word is the **anchor** we can hold on to in the times of the **storms** in our life. God's word:

- **is a comfort** – Psalm 57:1-3 (NKVJ) *[1] God, be merciful to me. Be kind because my soul trusts in you. I have come to you for protection, while the trouble passes. [2] I pray to God Most High for help, and he takes care of me completely! [3] From heaven he helps me and saves me. He will punish the one who attacks me. Selah God will remain loyal to me and send his love to protect me.*

- **is a reminder of God's promises** – Matthew 11:28 (NKJV) – *[28] Come to Me, all you who labor and are heavy laden, and I will give you rest.*

- **is a compass for our lives** – Proverbs 3:5-6 (NKJV) – *[5] Trust in the Lord with all your heart, And lean not on your own understanding; [6] In all your ways acknowledge Him, And He shall direct your paths.*

- **teaches us how the God works** – 1 Cor. 10:1-13 (NKJV) - ... *[11] Now all these things happened to them as examples, and they were written for our admonition, upon whom the ends of the ages have come. [12] Therefore let him who thinks he stands take heed lest he fall. [13] No temptation has overtaken you except such as is common to man; but God is faithful, who will not allow you to be tempted beyond what you are able, but with the temptation will also make the way of escape, that you may be able to bear it. [12] Therefore let him who thinks he stands take heed lest he fall. [13] No temptation has overtaken you except such as is common* *to man; but God is faithful, who will not allow you to be tempted beyond what you are able, but with the temptation will also make the way of escape, that you may be able to bear it* (click this link to read the entire scripture passage).

God's Word does us absolutely no good sitting on a shelf in our closet just gathering dust. For His Word to truly be **An Anchor in the Time of the Storm** we have to read it, meditate on it, believe it, apply it to our life and obey it.

Reflection:

In the days following the 2012 Presidential election many will still be facing the storm of their life as they deal with the damage resulting from Superstorm Sandy. These folks "are/will be" in great need of an **anchor** as they recover. Jesus and the Bible are that **anchor**.

I sang my first church solo at the Sunset Hills Baptist Church in Richmond, Virginia when I was a six-year-old. I was a member of the children's choir and we sang along with the adults in a Christmas special. Believe it or not, that solo was "Oh Holy Night," quite a difficult song for a six-year-old. That experience started a lifetime of singing solos at church services, weddings and funerals. One of my favorite solos of all time is "*The Anchor Holds*" with lyrics by Ray Boltz. Watch the presentation of this very special song originally released in 1995.

The Anchor Holds

I have journeyed
Through the long dark night
Out on the open sea

By faith alone
Sight unknown
And yet his eyes were watching me.

CHORUS
The anchor holds
Though the ship is battered
the anchor holds
Though the sails are torn
I have fallen on my knees
As I faced the raging seas
The anchor holds
In spite of the storm

I've had visions
I've had dreams
I've even held them in my hand
But I never knew
They would slip right through
Like they were only grains of sand

CHORUS
I have been young
But I am older now
And there has been beauty these eyes have seen
But it was in the night
Through the storms of my life
Oh that's where God proved his love to me

When I was nine years old our family moved back to Georgia
from Virginia where my father had been transferred in the
midst of World War II. We attended White Oak Hills Baptist
Church, then located in Decatur, Georgia. I accepted Christ as
my Savior when I was twelve years old and began my spiritual
journey toward maturity in that conservative Southern Baptist

church. Julian Wilson was our Music Director at that time. Our youth choir had more than sixty members and Mr. Wilson challenged us with wonderfully arranged and often difficult anthems and hymns. Our youth Choir sang every Sunday Night and the church crowds were large. We sang Hymns and a few choruses back then ... all with piano and organ ... and to me all of the hymns were **praise** music!

In Times Like These

Ruth Caye Jones – Mother Jones (1902-1972)

Dwelling a moment on one hymn in particular that I really didn't have enough appreciation for as a teenager is an appropriate way to wrap up this article. Ruth Caye Jones (Mother Jones, 1902-1972) penned the words and music to "*In Times Like These*" in 1944 in London in the midst of World War II. How appropriate! Times were really tough then as millions were giving their lives for the sake of freedom. Germany had continually bombarded London and was still on the offensive. That would soon change. Listen and watch George Beverly Shea present "*In Times Like These*" during a 1984 Billy Graham Crusade ... a wonderful and inspiring message of how Jesus and the Bible are *Your* **Anchor in the Time of the Storm**.

In Times Like These

Words and Music by Ruth Caye Jones

In times like these you need a Savior;
In times like these you need an anchor.
Be very sure, be very sure
Your anchor holds and grips the Solid Rock!

In times like these you need the Bible;
In times like these oh be not idle.
Be very sure, be very sure
Your anchor holds and grips the Solid Rock!

In times like these, I have a Savior;
In times like these, I have an anchor.
I'm very sure, I'm very sure
My anchor holds and grips the Solid Rock!

Chorus:
This Rock is Jesus, Yes, He's the One;
This Rock is Jesus, the only One!
Be very sure, be very sure
Your anchor holds and grips the Solid Rock!

Links for additional study and reflection:

- Our Anchor in Times of Storm, Dr. Charles Stanley

Related Music:

- The Anchor Holds – Ray Boltz
- In Times Like These – George Beverly Shea
- He Restoreth My Soul – The Good News
- He'll Hold My Hand – The Good News

03 – Hope and Change

Background:

In the year of 2008, leading up to the USA presidential election, the airwaves were filled with speeches and advertisements trumpeting the slogan **"Hope and Change."** This catch phrase did indeed capture the imagination and support for the Democratic party and helped to catapult the Democrats into majority positions in the Senate and the House, and vaulted Barack Hussein Obama into the Presidency.

Looking back now with 20/20 hindsight, the campaign slogan of **"Hope and Change"** has proven to be primarily that ... a slogan. There was little explanation or substance provided in advance for how the **"Hope and Change"** would be implemented and it is still difficult for the average voter to grasp the details of what the slogan embodied.

At the beginning of President Obama's term in office the country was in a significant economic crisis. President George W. Bush had previously signed the Troubled Asset Relief Program (TARP) into law on October 3, 2008 to deal with the sub-prime mortgage crisis. Through additional legislation and executive orders President Obama's administration continued to deal with broader economic problems. Two of the three major U.S. auto manufacturers were ushered through a government managed bankruptcy of sorts where the government gave priority to union workers over the usual process of treating bondholders and creditors first in the settlement. The Democratic majority in the House and Senate also passed a $900 billion financial "stimulus" package for what was termed "shovel ready projects" only later to admit that the projects were not so shovel ready after all.

On March 23, 2010 President Obama signed into law a massive and politically divisive health care reform bill known as the Patient Protection and Affordable Care Act (PPACA), commonly called Obamacare. Not one Republican in the House or Senate voted in favor of PPACA.

With a significant Tea Party movement, the Republican party took back control of the House in the 2010 elections and a state of legislative gridlock emerged in January 2011. Since then very little of substance has **changed**. The two political parties and the U.S. citizenry are sharply divided over future direction and most of 2012 has been consumed by political campaigning. A national budget has not been passed for four years. Government spending is out of control. The country faces another financial crisis often called a "fiscal cliff" and another major recession in 2013 if the legislative branch can not agree on at least temporary financial reforms by the end of 2012. After nearly four years of President Obama's administration, the U.S. is still struggling with significant issues such as:

- a massive $16.2 trillion national debt forecast for 2012 at $141,435 per taxpayer, $51,508 per citizen (see U.S. National Debt Clock)
- an unacceptable employment level for our citizens – with a total workforce of 143.2 million and a total population of 314.6 million: currently 8.4% with 12.0 million official unemployed; 15.8% with 22.7 million actual unemployed (see U.S. National Debt Clock)
- nearly 1 in 7 (47.1 million) Americans on food stamps costing $72 billion in 2011, up $40 billion in last three years
- 50% of recent college graduates jobless forcing many parents to continue their support
- a huge divide between Democrats and Republicans causing legislative gridlock
- a continuing war in Afghanistan costing precious lives of so many young Americans
- governmental chaos in Libya, Egypt, Syria and Yemen with problems brewing in others
- the Islamic Republic of Iran closer to a nuclear weapon with an outspoken President committed to the destruction of Israel
- an administration advocating support for same-sex marriage and the continuation of abortion on demand

It is no wonder to me that the slogan of **"Hope and Change"** struck so many chords with the American public in 2008. We were, and now are, a sick society drowning in our individual and collective sin … wanting to believe. Unfortunately, our government and our people are trying to make significant **changes** on their own by placing their confidence for **"Hope and Change"** in man without the guidance of Almighty God. True and Godly **"change"** will never spring from man alone. What our citizenry and our government urgently need to do is seek the Lord God and turn from our wicked ways. It is only in and of God that we will find true "**Hope and Change**."

Scripture: (all scripture NASB unless otherwise noted)

Galatians 1:15-24 – *15 But when God, who had set me apart even from my mother's womb and called me through His grace, was pleased 16 to reveal His Son in me so that I might preach Him among the Gentiles, I did not immediately consult with flesh and blood, 17 nor did I go up to Jerusalem to those who were apostles before me; but I went away to Arabia, and returned once more to Damascus.18 Then three years later I went up to Jerusalem to become acquainted with Cephas, and stayed with him fifteen days. 19 But I did not see any other of the apostles except James, the Lord's brother. 20 (Now in what I am writing to you, I assure you before God that I am not lying.) 21 Then I went into the regions of Syria and Cilicia. 22 I was still unknown by sight to the churches of Judea which were in Christ; 23 but only, they kept hearing, **"He who once persecuted us is now preaching the faith which he once tried to destroy."** 24 And they were glorifying God because of me.*

Matthew 7:13-14 – *13 "Enter through the narrow gate; for the gate is wide and **the way is broad that leads to destruction**, and there are many who enter through it. 14 For the gate is small and the way is narrow that leads to life, and there are few who find it.*

Psalm 62:5 - *My soul, wait in silence for God only, For my **hope** is from Him.*

2 Corinthians 3:4-5 - *4 Such confidence we have through Christ toward God. 5 Not that we are adequate in ourselves to consider anything as coming from ourselves, but our adequacy is from God, ...*

2 Corinthians 5:17 – *Therefore if any man is in Christ, he is a new creature; the old things passed away; behold, new things have come.*

Romans 12:2 – *And do not be conformed to this world, but be transformed {**changed**} by the renewing of your mind, that you may prove what the will of God is, that which is good and acceptable and perfect.*

Acts 3:17-21 - [17] *"And now, brethren, I know that you **acted in ignorance, just as your rulers did also**. [18] But the things which God announced beforehand by the mouth of all the prophets, that His Christ would suffer, He has thus fulfilled. [19] **Therefore repent and return, so that your sins may be wiped away, in order that times of refreshing may come from the presence of the Lord;** [20] and that He may send Jesus, the Christ appointed for you, [21] whom heaven must receive until the period of restoration of all things about which God spoke by the mouth of His holy prophets from ancient time.*

Discussion:

In Galatians 1:15-24 Paul the Apostle describes in dramatic detail how God transformed his life. Paul was known as Saul prior to his conversion experience (Acts 9:1-22; Acts 22:3-16; Acts 26:9-18) on the Road to Damascus. Saul was a zealous Pharisee dedicated to the persecution and even the death of many early disciples of Jesus in the area of Jerusalem. When Saul met Jesus and became a dedicated follower of Christ, his whole life **changed**. His **hope** was now centered on the cross of Jesus where He paid the price for our sins through His crucifixion, burial and resurrection thus conquering sin and death. Jesus was now Paul's only cause and he spent the rest of his life leading others to "**Hope and Change**" by accepting Christ as Savior.

While Paul **changed** from a Christian killer to a Christian church founding preacher, your need for **change** may not be that dramatic. Christ can **change** your heart, outlook and outcome. Real **"change"** requires true repentance and a willingness to give up old worldly ways for dealing with life's issues. Just think back to Old Testament times … Israel was blessed when they followed God's instruction and they suffered greatly when they didn't. Partial repentance is not enough. We can't pick and choose the portions of God's Word with which we want to agree. There is no bargaining with God. It is His way or our way. His way leads to real **hope and change**. Man's way is the path to destruction (Matthew 7:13-14). Christians should live in a constant state of repentance placing their **hope** only in the Lord (Psalm 62:5) and not in man (2 Corinthians 3:4-5).

Paul taught in 2 Corinthians 5:17 – *Therefore if any man is in Christ, he is a new creature; the old things passed away; behold, new things have come.* And further in Romans 12:2 that we are not to be conformed to the world's ways but rather be *"transformed {changed} by the renewing of your mind, that you may prove what the will of God is, that which is good and acceptable and perfect.*

Acts chapter 3 records the healing of the lame beggar and Peter's second sermon after God sent the Holy Spirit on the believers on the Day of Pentecost (see Acts 2:1-13). In Acts 3:17 Peter preached to the "brethren" that they had *"acted in ignorance, just as your rulers did."* In verse 18 Peter went on to say **ALL** that God had promised them was/is fulfilled through Jesus. And in verse 19, they should *"Therefore repent and return, so that your sins may be wiped away, in order that times of refreshing may come from the presence of the Lord."* This then is the true definition to "**Hope and Change.**" It is not of man … it is only of God through our

Savior Jesus Christ, the Messiah!! Praise God from whom all blessings flow!!

Reflection:

It is easy to put our faith in the wrong people, the wrong places and the wrong things. The only real agent for "Hope and Change" is Almighty God Himself. True, we are created in God's image and He uses man to accomplish His purpose. But without God's guidance people, places and things are useless in solving both our individual and collective problems. What we desperately need in the U.S. are God fearing, God serving public servants ... servants committed to the Word of God ... servants who stand on the promises of God ... servants who seek God's understanding and God's will ... servants who don't substitute man's ways for God's ways ... servants who are set apart from the world but in the world ... servants willing to do what is right in the sight of God ... servants who are thankful ... servants who are prayerful ... servants who are submitted, giving and humble. That's a mouthful, but I submit that is what the U.S. needs to solve the huge problems we face as a nation.

The Bible teaches that God is in control ALL of the time, that He is ALL knowing, and He is ALL powerful. He has the answers to ALL of our problems. Can you name me one person, place or thing that can compare to God? I don't think so! Then why would you put your trust elsewhere?

I encourage you to prayerfully consider your vote in the upcoming Presidential election on November 6, 2012. Pray that God will place upon your heart His decision for you. Don't trust yourself or anyone else without consulting God.

Romney Ryan

Obama Biden

The U.S. is at a turning point. Our future and the future of our children, grandchildren and succeeding generations weigh in the balance. Above all, put your trust in God and not in man for the "**Hope and Change**" our nation so urgently needs.

On a personal level, you may feel that you cannot make the **changes** required to become a follower of God. Some think they are too sinful to be pardoned. Some try to give up their sinful ways by themselves only to miserably fail over and over again. Take comfort in knowing that God will help you make the **changes**. Turn your life over to Him and He will save you and give you eternal life. By accepting Jesus Christ as his Savior Paul made an unbelievable change from Christian killer to Christian preacher. Jesus can help you make similar changes … no matter how deep you have descended into sin.

I invite you to view a YouTube presentation of one of my favorite songs by the famous southern gospel quartet, The Cathedrals, recorded in their final year together in 1999. The name of the song is "He Made A Change." If you have the time, you might also want to listen to the 1990 recording by The Good News, The Plan of Salvation. I believe this is a perfect way to reflect on the message of this article.

References for Additional Study and Reflection:

The Cathedrals

He Made a Change – a 1999 video by The Cathedrals, a southern gospel quartet; one of my favorite songs of all time featuring Ernie Haas (tenor), Scott Fowler (baritone), Glenn Payne (lead), George Younce (bass) and Roger Bennett (piano).

The Plan of Salvation – a 1990 recording by The Good News, a southern Gospel Quartet consisting of Mark Fuller (piano), Charles Thomas (baritone), Arnold Johnson (bass), Jim Davenport (tenor), and Ray Shaw (lead). Listen to more from The Good News at this link.

04 – So Where Is My Choice? A Father's Day Message on the Sanctity of Life

Prologue:

Today is Father's Day, June 17, 2012. I've been thinking about my father today ... in particular I have been thinking about a time in our lives when my father was my hero. I was twelve years old. My mother had a serious case of tuberculosis. At that time tuberculosis was highly contagious and the state required that Mom be isolated at Battey State Hospital in Rome, Georgia some 75 miles from our home in Decatur, Georgia. Almost every Sunday my Dad would drive to Rome to see my mother and he would take me along. Regulations forbid me to be anywhere near my mother. Dad had such a privilege, but he had to wear a clinical mask and had limited contact with my Mom. I would sit in the car, preferably in the shade, and wait on his return. When my Mom felt up to it she would go to a window and wave to me. That was the only way I could see her for more than a year.

Administration Building ca. 1955, Photo courtesy of John Donovan

When school was out, my younger sister Barbara stayed with my older sister Patricia at her home in Detroit. My Dad and I "batched" it together for that summer. He cooked, got me ready for YMCA day camp, made me a lunch, and took me to the pickup spot for the bus to pick me up for day camp. He then drove twenty miles to his job and worked all day. He usually got home late in the evening since he was one of the store managers. I had learned to swim at the day camp and was so excited about it that I wanted him to see what I could do. So, after he got home and even before he made dinner he would take me to the swimming pool to show off for him. In the fall Barbara came home to go back to school. My dad was a wonderful Dad to us. He somehow managed to find time to take me quail hunting on his day off. He generally did everything at home my Mom had previously done. Looking back I don't know how he kept the pace. Eventually Dad had his half-sister, Ruby Akins, come to live with us to handle some of the household duties. Those were tough times for my younger sister, my Aunt, and particularly for my Mom and Dad.

Wow! In recalling those times I realize that I never gave enough credit to my Dad during his lifetime for the sacrifices he made during that two-year period. My thinking has always been mostly about my Mom and how she suffered. I really missed her, and she missed all of us deeply. It would have been easy for my Dad to give up, to decrease rather than increase his time with me, to complain ... but he didn't. My Dad loved me and I knew that until the day he died. He loved me even before I was born and he still loves me from his home in Heaven with our Heavenly Father.

This is **my** body...

so where is **my CHOICE**?

www.facebook.com/IStand4Life

What if this were you?

These memories caused me to hearken back to a previous post I wrote in 2011 on The Sanctity of Life and Abortion. One of the thoughts that crossed my mind was … "What if my mother and father had decided to have an abortion when she was pregnant with me … there would be no love between me and my mother and father, no life at all, no dearly beloved wife of 49 years, no children, no grandchildren, no great-grandchildren." What if my parents had said, "we just can't afford another child right now and any way it's not really a baby that's inside Lottie, it's just a fetus, part of her body, and her decision to do what she wanted to do with me. Besides we are right in the middle of World War II and we should be focused on helping our country … not on raising another baby." Of course, this scenario would have ignored the truth about abortion that is that abortion is tantamount to murder and millions of unborn babies are murdered each year.

While a number of people were following my blog when I first started writing early in 2011, there are many new readers now who may have not read my original post "On the Sanctity of

Life and Abortion." So bear with me as I reproduce it in its entirety within the context of this article.

Background:

Friends, I am burdened by the way that we so easily brush off the "lawful" murder/sacrifice of unborn children in the US. I believe that God will place our complacency toward this genocide alongside that of what Hitler did to the Jews through their mass slaughter. Since abortion has been "lawful" in the US, over 40 million unborn babies have never seen the light of day. As so many consider the decision to abort a child solely that of the mother, I wonder if those same people could agree that it is also the mother's right to kill her baby after it is born. Our law calls that murder, but the abortion/murder decision is the sole privilege of the mother. I find this totally inconsistent from a human law standpoint. More important it is clear that the Bible teaches that abortion is murder. Would you pray during this "Sanctity of Life" week that God will intervene in this terrible genocide and allow man to truly see the error of his ways? May God forgive us as Christians for such complacency and urge us to tell everyone we know that as a society we will pay for the consequences of our collective sin.

The comments below are summarized from a Sunday School lesson I first taught to a married couple's class in 1994 and have updated recently. They offer some biblical background on valuing human life. Unfortunately, it has only gotten worse in these past 17 years.

Discussion:

During the 20th century, humans have lived through the greatest period of change in the history of the world. Discoveries by natural science and countless new technical inventions have provided us with previously unheard of luxuries such as personal computers, iPhones, iPods, iPads, etc. However, during this same period, moral and spiritual values that withstood the test of the ages have gone into major decline. Our spiritual senses have been dulled primarily due to the influence of materialism. Everyday conduct that was condemned by previous generations has been commonly accepted as a life-style by today's generation.

Particularly noticeable in today's society is the *lack of value placed upon human life.* Just look at some of the evidences that the value is cheap: the rising murder rate; the advent of car-jacking and senseless killings; the controversy over euthanasia and voluntary suicide; the violence and illicit sex which fills our streets, movies, television, and communities; and perhaps the most telling of all, the millions of aborted babies who were never given a chance to be what God planned for them to be when they were conceived.

Sadly, many adults prefer to change the subject when the topic of sanctity of life and abortion arises. Most prefer to let others deal with the abortion issue. But unfortunately, there is no way we can avoid this crucial issue. Directly or indirectly, each of us is affected by the decisions enacted by our government in relation to abortion. There really is no middle ground on this issue with God. Let's look to the Bible for God's directive.

Scripture:

I.   All human life comes from God (Gen. 1:27).

Genesis 1 (NIV)

27 So God created man in His own image, in the image of God he created him; male and female he created them.

The Hebrew word for "create" is used **only of God**. It expresses the incomparable creative activity of God. While it is possible for people to invent or even to discover, **only God can create**. Consider how God made the first human Adam. (Gen 2:7) God breathed into man the "breath of life", and that is what makes man unique on this earth. John 4:24 tells us that "God is spirit, and His worshipers must worship in spirit and in truth." If we are created in His image, then we too are spirit. Jeremiah 1:5 tells us about how God views the pre-born child by stating *"Before I formed you in the womb I knew you, before you were born I set you apart; I appointed you as a prophet to the nations."* A person's worth to God does not depend on age, gender, or nationality.

II. Jesus instructs Christians to influence society (Matt. 5:13-16) (all scriptures are NIV unless otherwise noted).

13 "You are the salt of the earth. But if the salt loses its saltiness, how can it be made salty again? It is no longer good for anything, except to be thrown out and trampled underfoot. 14 You are the light of the world. A town built on a hill cannot be hidden. 15 Neither do people light a lamp and put it under a bowl. Instead they put it on its stand, and it gives light to everyone in the house. 16 In the same way, let your light shine before others, that they may see your good deeds and glorify your Father in heaven.

Christians are the "salt" of the earth. We lose our "saltiness" when we do not stand up for what is right. Eventually the lack of saltiness leads to the loss of purpose. We are also to be visible in the world (light), not hidden away from view. Christians must express their convictions regarding crucial moral issues such as abortion, pornography, child abuse, homosexuality, and substance abuse. I contend it is "right" for a Christian to take a stand and strongly urge those in government to correct the wrongs we see in our society. Christians must take the initiative to be salt and light on the abortion issue.

III. Jesus calls us to a new attitude concerning the value of Human Life (Matt. 5:21-22).

21 You have heard that it was said to the people long ago, 'You shall not murder, and anyone who murders will be subject to judgment.' 22 But I tell you that anyone who is angry with a brother or sister will be subject to judgment. Again, anyone who says to a brother or sister, 'Raca,' is answerable to the court. And anyone who says, 'You fool!' will be in danger of the fire of hell.

The sixth commandment tells us that murder is wrong. How can people seem to have great understanding of the commandments of God and fail to see this command as it relates to the pre-born baby? Jesus speaks about man's outward appearances and inward thoughts in verse 22 and tells us that we will be subject to judgment. It is clear from the scripture that man be judged by God on the abortion issue. Regardless of what you think about abortion, God's position is clear. It is murder. The term "Raca" is a reproach used by the Jews in the time of Christ, meaning "worthless." The Jews used it as a word of contempt. It is derived from a root meaning "to spit." Is there really a question in your mind on where Jesus stands on the issue of abortion?

IV.   Jesus commands us to live with sexual purity (Matt. 5:27-28).

27 You have heard that it was said, 'You shall not commit adultery.' 28 But I tell you that anyone who looks at a woman lustfully has already committed adultery with her in his heart.

President Jimmy Carter got in trouble with the news media for admitting that he had "lusted" in his heart and for stating that he was a "born again" Christian. The teaching of Jesus clearly indicates that inward lust is sin ... not just the outward act of adultery. This is different from what was being taught and practiced by the Jewish leadership based on their interpretation of the scriptures. Sexual attraction was created by God and is to be limited to the confines of marriage. Lust is the product of Satan and has been adopted by the sinful nature of man. Lust has been marginalized and popularized in our modern-day through movies, television and advertising. At every turn we are bombarded with messages that encourage us to accept sinful and sexual pleasures as a normal lifestyle. Couples live together outside of marriage in open defiance of God's word. Countless Fortune 500 companies use sex as the central point of their message to sell their product. Ultimately the abortion issue just blends into our tolerance for immorality. In 1 Corinthians 9:27 Paul calls Christians to be accountable for their conduct and "bring their bodies into subjection."

V.   Jesus demands that we value all human life (Matt. 5:43-45a).

43 You have heard that it was said, 'Love your neighbor and hate your enemy.' 44 But I tell you, love your enemies and pray for those who persecute you, 45 that you may be children of your Father in heaven."

Christian love as described by Jesus compels us to love all individuals, even our enemies. Such love includes protecting those individuals who cannot defend themselves. Some might argue that Christians have no responsibility in changing the attitude of our nation toward abortion. I contend that Christians have a deep responsibility to defend the un-born child, to counsel the unwed mother that there are alternatives to abortion, to counsel a mother who has had an abortion that God will forgive her of her heinous sin, and to persuade a couple who is considering abortion not to terminate an unplanned pregnancy.

Reflection:

If all of human life comes from God, will you follow God's example and consider all life precious and sacred? How will you as a Christian influence our society? It is not enough to sit back and let someone else do it for you. A healthy and growing relationship with God means that our attitudes and actions must change to promote the value and worth of all people, particularly those who never get a chance to be born for the first time.

The link below will take you to a video posted on Facebook by the Valley Baptist Church in Bakersfield, California. It is a wonderful depiction of the unborn child's life cycle. I urge you to spend the few minutes it takes to view it and then pray that God will embolden you to take action about the pitiful human tragedy "we the people" are allowing to continue by "law" in the United States of America.

http://www.facebook.com/video/video.php?v=488452018044

Epilogue:

The opening portion of this article dealt with a time in my life that had a great deal to do with shaping the rest of my life. My life-values were already established when my mother got sick with tuberculosis. But I can tell you that the example my father set for me during that two-year ordeal had a lot to do with cementing them into my fabric for the rest of my life. I loved both of my parents dearly for the rest of their lives. My father passed away in 1986 at 76 years old after nearly a year-long illness brought on by a stroke. He had a sweet spirit and he loved me. I learned so much from my father. He was an honest man who had his faults, but then don't all of us. The thing I remember the most about him was that he was a friend to all, but mostly to me. I thank God for both my earthly and my Heavenly Father.

My mother lived on to be 91. She and my father were married for 57 years. I will never forgot how hard they fought together to beat the tuberculosis and return the family to normalcy. And I thank God that they did not abort me in 1943 when it was not "convenient" nor "affordable" to have another baby!

What if this was you? Would you want your parent to abort you? Unborn babies have no choice!

05 – On Child Sacrifice

Background:

I can't get this topic off of my mind … and it troubles me how calloused we are as a society to allow this to be the law of the land without major outrage. What troubles me even more is the continuous slide by our nation into total immorality. Our nation teeters on the collapse of our balanced form of government founded in 1776. Our forefathers saw fit to create a republic consisting of three branches of government … the executive, the legislative and the judicial. Counter to popular opinion we are not a democracy as so many have been taught to believe through our governmental supplied public school system. By design, the three branches are supposed to independently counter-balance each other. By and large, the system has worked very well for our citizens. However, recent decisions by the Supreme Court during this early summer session and the recently announced presidential support for same-sex marriage provide further validation of the mess that we are in after only 236 years of existence as a sovereign nation. Our downward spiral continues. But that is not exactly the subject of this article. My hope is that by the end of this article you will see how our governmental mess relates to the stated topic, *On Child Sacrifice*.

Late this afternoon my wife drove us from our Lookout mountain home in Alabama to our favorite restaurant in all of the world, The Canyon Grill, located on Lookout mountain in the New Salem, Georgia community above the valley town of Trenton, Georgia.

The restaurant is located near the Cloudland Canyon State Park. Perhaps you have been there. What a beautiful view of God's creation from the top of that canyon! Many of you know that I have had health problems for some time which have kept me near to home most of the time. But I am feeling better these days and we ventured the fifty mile round trip to enjoy a delicious and delightful dinner.

While we were waiting for our food we couldn't help but overhear the conversation of the six folks seated at the table next to us. In a loud and firm voice the mature gray-headed gentleman said something like this: "Well, it comes down to this ... if you favor same-sex marriage and abortion, then vote for the democrats. If you don't, then vote for the republicans." That thought struck home with me and I immediately turned my mind to the thinking that I had been doing earlier this week about this article. I believe that God allowed me to hear the man's comment in order to cement into my mind and record the contents of this writing.

Scripture: (all NKJV unless otherwise noted)

2 Kings 23:10 – *And he defiled Topheth, which is in the Valley of the Son of Hinnom, that no man might make his son or his daughter pass through the fire to Molech.*

Jeremiah 7:31 - *And they have built the high places of Tophet, which is in the Valley of the Son of Hinnom, to burn their sons and their daughters in the fire, which I did not command, nor did it come into My heart.*

Jeremiah 19:12-15 - *¹² Thus I will do to this place," says the Lord, "and to its inhabitants, and make this city like Tophet. ¹³ And the houses of Jerusalem and the houses of the kings of Judah shall be defiled like the place of Tophet, because of all the houses on whose roofs they have burned incense to all the host of heaven, and poured out drink offerings to other gods."'" ¹⁴ Then Jeremiah came from Tophet, where the Lord had sent him to prophesy; and he stood in the court of the Lord's house and said to all the people, ¹⁵ "Thus says the Lord of hosts, the God of Israel: 'Behold, I will bring on this city and on all her towns all the doom that I have pronounced against it, because they have **stiffened their necks** that they might not hear My words.'"*

Isaiah 30:31-33 - *³¹ For through the voice of the Lord Assyria will be beaten down, As He strikes with the rod. ³² And in every place where the staff of punishment passes, Which the Lord lays on him, It will be with tambourines and harps; And in battles of brandishing He will fight with it. ³³ For Tophet was established of old, Yes, for the king it is prepared. He has made it deep and large; Its pyre is fire with much wood; The breath of the Lord, like a stream of brimstone, Kindles it.*

Matthew 5:22) – *But I say to you that whoever is angry with his brother without a cause shall be in danger of the judgment. And whoever says to his brother, 'Raca!' shall be in danger of the council. But whoever says, 'You fool!' shall be in danger of hell fire* (Gehenna).

Matthew 18:9 – *And if your eye causes you to sin, pluck it out and cast it from you. It is better for you to enter into life with one eye, rather than having two eyes, to be cast into hell fire.*

Discussion:

If you know anything about ancient history you will know that many societies often practiced the ritual sacrifice of humans and even their children to gain the favor of their gods. We often think of this as being related to primitive or tribal people with barbaric lifestyles. Child sacrifice was practiced in Old Testament days by many of the Israel's neighbors and mentioned multiple times in the Bible. Those who worshiped the god Molech in the *Valley of Hinnom* (2 Kings 23:10) allowed their children to be burned with fire (Jeremiah 7:31). The valley of Hinnom runs east-west and lies on the southern side of the city of Jerusalem. The cultic site referred to as Tophet (sometimes Topheth) was in this valley. A note in *The Thomas Nelson Chronological Bible* relates that the Biblical prophets often mentioned the **fire of Tophet** in describing Almighty God's judgment on those who were not faithful to Him. For example, see Jeremiah 19:12-15 where the prophet says that God would make Jerusalem and the towns around it like Tophet — like a place of burning — because they had *"**stiffened their necks**"* against God's will. Isaiah also pronounced that a similar punishment would fall on Assyria (Isaiah 30:31-33). Isaiah said that God's anger would be like a *"flame of devouring fire,"* the fire of Tophet. The flame would be all-consuming and more than adequate to punish all offenders. Verse 33 closes with the statement that *"... the breath of the Lord, like a stream of brimstone kindles it."*

By New Testament times the *Valley of Hinnom* was referred to by the Aramaic word *"gehinna*m" which was also known in Greek as *Gehenna,* or the "hell fire" (see Matthew 5:22). Jesus warned about the Gehenna, or the "hell fire," in Matthew 18:9 inferring that Gehenna would be a fiery judgment like the fire of Tophet as proclaimed by Isaiah.

Reflection:

So, here's where I tie all of this together. I think most will agree that "child sacrifice" for any reason is just plain "murder." That, of course, violates one of God's Ten Commandments. In my mind and in accordance with what the Bible teaches I have to ask this question – **How is abortion different from "child sacrifice" and thus murder?** Aborting a child to me is equivalent to child sacrifice and murder. Murder is equated in the scripture with unlawful killing resulting in bloodguilt. So we have passed and upheld "laws" that make abortion lawful and not resulting in bloodguilt. So what is bloodguilt anyway? Follow this link to a Jewish explanation of bloodguilt as presented in numerous Old Testament scriptures. The New Testament validates the Old Testament teachings. If you have doubts about the validity of my statement, then refer to the following scriptures: Matthew 23:30-35, Matthew 27:4, Luke 11:50-51, Romans 3:15, Revelation 6:10, Revelation 18:24. In particular, abortion results in the shedding of innocent blood and is viewed as a direct offense against God as our Creator since all men are created in His image.

So how can so many blatantly ignore that the "murder" of an unborn baby, a child, or an adult for that matter, is totally against what God and the Holy Bible teach us about the sanctity of life? Yet all three branches of our government ... executive, legislative and judicial ... have proposed, discussed, passed and verified under close examination that abortion is legal in the USA. As I view it, this means that by mans' law we have allowed the "child sacrifice" of more than fifty-four million (54,000,000) babies under the banner of legal abortion since Roe v. Wade was passed in 1973. How staggering and sickening!! That is more than the population of any state in the Union by a long shot. For example consider the population of California (approximately 36 million), Texas (23 million) and New York (approximately 19 million). If you want to look at the abortion statistics compiled by the NRLC I have quoted above yourself, then follow the link. Randall K. O'Bannon, Ph.D. wrote an article (Fifty Million Lost Lives Since 1973) in January 2008 containing a profound statement I reproduce below without further comment because I can't say it any better in my own words:

"By the time you read this sentence, America will have passed a tragic, momentous, and most sobering milestone. Within a day or two of January 22, 2008, the 35th anniversary of Roe v. Wade, baby number 50,000,000 will have been sacrificed on the altar of Roe v. Wade.

The magnitude of the killing is staggering. Fifty million represents a population greater than any state, greater than California (36 million), greater than the next two largest states—Texas and New York— combined (23 million and 19 million, respectively). In fact, if you combined the entire populations of all of the 25 states with the fewest people, it still would not equal 50 million.

Of course, the issue isn't numbers. Each abortion represents at least one lost life and what may be a deeply wounded woman's soul. Families, too, suffer, and society itself pays a dear price, with lost innovation, productivity, and creativity.

How many great books, symphonies, films have been lost? How many profitable businesses never came to be? What if we aborted the child who would have found the cure for cancer? How much love and laughter has the world been deprived of?"

How can our government be guilty of passing so many laws that are so absurdly immoral and ungodly? I believe our forefathers, were they alive today, would be loudly and passionately voicing their opinions about the lunacy of many of the "laws" we have enacted that go directly against Almighty God's directives. Some of you reading this may be thinking that the separation of church and state means that our laws do not have to follow the principles found in the Bible. I don't go so far as to say that we should use the rule of law to mandate a religion. In fact, I believe quite the opposite. The first amendment to the US constitution reads:

"Congress shall make no law respecting an establishment of religion, or prohibiting the free exercise thereof; or abridging the freedom of speech, or of the press; or the right of the people peaceably to assemble, and to petition the Government for a redress of grievances."

But common sense should tell you that much of what we have legislated into law and are practicing as a nation to be "politically correct" is not good for our country's future and is an abomination to God. If you have followed my writings for any amount of time, then you know that one of my constant themes is that when people and nations go against God and the Bible's teachings, there are both earthly and eternal consequences that will have to be paid for such unGodliness. The USA will suffer the consequences of ignoring God's commands. There is no doubt in my mind about that. Our leaders who take us to that immoral ground will also suffer. And there is no doubt in my mind about that either.

As a people the majority in the USA seem to have "*stiffened their necks*" against God's will when it comes to abortion. God will not let this continue without major repercussions. God's anger will be like a "*flame of devouring fire,*" the fire of Tophet. The flame will be all-consuming and more than adequate to punish all offenders. "*... The breath of the Lord, (will be) like a stream of brimstone (that) kindles it* (Isaiah 30:33)." How are we that different from the primitive or tribal people who practice child sacrifice? I say ... we are not that different at all. We have the bloodguilt of more than 54 million souls on our hands. How many more abortions will it take to wake us up? And as a final note, I will be voting Republican in the November elections.

Not Human?

Child sacrifice to Molech

Child sacrifice to Canaanite gods

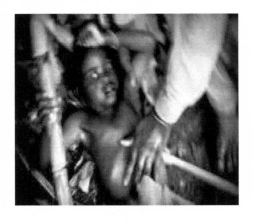

Child sacrifice in modern day Uganda

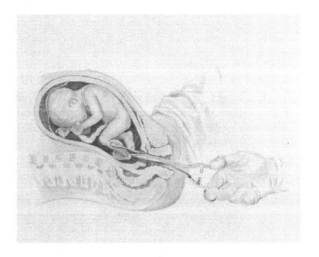

Child Sacrifice in modern-day USA! 54 million since 1973 …. and counting!! Dear God, how can you ever forgive us for sacrificing our children to "Molech" in the fire of Tophet?

06 – Calling Evil Good

Background:

Have you come to a peaceful co-existence with evil? In today's permissive society it is often difficult to tell the difference between what is "good" and what is "evil". For example, what was once called the sin of sodomy is now called sexual orientation ... and we have passed legislation to elevate that to being "normal". Over time, our modern-day society has perverted the definition of what is good to the point where more and more evil is defined as good. Many churches walk a fine line between God's way and man's way making it difficult to distinguish them from the world.

Sadly, our world is full of "misguided" people ... those who are hooked on drugs, those who fall into a life of crime, those who take the decisions of life and death into their own hands, those who falsely believe they can work their way to heaven, those who don't believe there are earthly consequences to their sin, those who ... you continue the thought. Even many of God's born-again children are misguided in their understanding of God's will and God's ways.

Tragically, far too many religious leaders wrongly lead their flocks into error by misusing, misquoting, and misapplication of God's Word. In many cases, the religious leader has another agenda other than God's truth. Most times the leader is simply following the dogma of their misguided religion. Extremists and terrorists give themselves over to suicide missions in the name of their "god" senselessly killing innocent men, women and children while following the perverted teachings of their zealous leaders.

I Was Made In God's Image – how could you abort me?

Under pressure from ardent lobbying groups or immoral leadership, governments all over the world have passed laws under the pretense that they are doing what is right and best for the populace. In past generations this led to the legalization of slavery and segregation and sanctioned as "good" many things that were actually "evil". For example, today's governments have legalized the killing of unborn babies (more than 53 million in the USA alone since Roe v. Wade, 1973) while prosecuting parents for the same crime after the child is born. China has adopted and is enforcing a one child policy which has resulted in an untold number of abortions. Parents are forced to abort their baby simply because they already have one child. Parents choose to abort their baby simply because it is the wrong sex. Girls are aborted more than boys in China so families can continue their bloodline through their sons.

In all of the cases mentioned above, man is attempting to redefine what is "good" and what is "evil" to suit his own desires bypassing God's definition of righteousness. God and His Holy Word, The Bible, have a lot to say about those who insist on *Calling Evil Good*.

Scripture: (all New King James Version (NKJV) unless otherwise noted)

Isaiah 5:20-21 - *²⁰ **Woe to those who call evil good, and good evil**; Who put darkness for light, and light for darkness; Who put bitter for sweet, and sweet for bitter! ²¹ **Woe to those who are wise in their own eyes**, And **prudent in their own sight!** ... ²⁴ Therefore, as the fire devours the stubble, And the flame consumes the chaff, So their **root will be as rottenness**, And their blossom will ascend like dust; **Because they have rejected the law of the Lord of hosts**, And despised the word of the Holy One of Israel.*

Hosea 14:9 – *Who is wise? Let him understand these things. Who is prudent? Let him know them. **For the ways of the Lord are right; The righteous walk in them**, But transgressors stumble in them.*

Galatians 6:7 – ***Do not be deceived, God is not mocked; for whatever a man sows, that he will also reap.***

Discussion:

Isaiah was one of the latter prophets who lived and prophesied in the eighth-century BC Kingdom of Judah. The primary message of the book of Isaiah (meaning *the salvation of the Lord*) is that salvation comes from God — not in any way or by anything of man. Salvation is the free gift of God. Praise God who is our Savior, Ruler and King.

In Isaiah 5:20-21 the prophet speaks *"Woe to those who call evil good and good evil..."* The word "**woe**" means a **condition of deep suffering** from misfortune, affliction, grief, ruinous calamity and in this case the prediction of the great suffering Judah would face at the hand of the Babylonians. Isaiah is passing along God's judgment on Judah for their excesses and for repeatedly disobeying His Word. Man cannot escape God's righteous judgment. Through Isaiah God said *"Woe to those who are wise in their own eyes, And prudent in their own sight!"* Wisdom is a gift from God. Man might think he is wise, but without God's gift man is greatly deceived about his supposed wisdom. God pronounces the consequences of those guilty of such sinfulness by saying *"So their root will be as rottenness, And their blossom will ascend like dust; Because they have rejected the law of the Lord of hosts, And despised the word of the Holy One of Israel."* (Isaiah 5:24)

How could God make it plainer for us? God is the author of all "good" and Satan is the great deceiver and the author of all "evil." There are consequences for evil. Evil is sin. Thus there are consequences for sin. I tend to over-complicate things at times so let's just reduce it to this: **Doing right is good, doing wrong is evil.** Hosea 14:9 asks *"Who is wise? Let him understand these things. Who is prudent? Let him know them. For the ways of the Lord are right; The righteous walk in them, But transgressors stumble in them.*

The Biblical principle of sowing and reaping can be applied here as well. In Galatians 6:7 Paul warns the Christian church at Galatia *"Do not be deceived, God is not mocked; for whatever a man sows, that he will also reap."*

Reflection:

I have often had discussions with my dear friend in Christ, Glen Crisler. Glen runs a successful business providing gainful employment, even in these difficult economic times, to a host of people. Glen is now in his late 70's and still going strong as he and his faithful wife Mary Elizabeth often travel over 50,000 miles each year visiting his job sites. Yet Glen and Mary Elizabeth are always in the house of the Lord at every opportunity. Glen unselfishly partners with his Pastor and church to further the cause of Christ.

Glen is a passionate soul winner having led so many to salvation and positively influenced so many others. Glen is a Godly man of integrity, honesty and compassion. Glen's leadership skills are remarkable. He has served as the Chairman of the Deacons in my home church for many, many years. In difficult situations Glen and I have often discussed options. Our conclusion in every instance over the years has been that we must do what is right in the sight of God, what is consistent with God's Word, no matter the consequences. Somehow that makes difficult situations much easier to handle. I love Glen and Mary and my wife Charlotte and I will enjoy an eternity in Heaven with these dear friends.

It is the Christian's job to sow what is right and shun what is wrong and to leave it up to God to do what is within His Holy will.

Dr. Charles Stanley in speaking in his sermon about America's Future says that '**Essentially, as a nation we have said, "We don't need You, God."** Dr. Stanley goes on to say that 'Man can pass laws legalizing ungodly behavior, but God's principles don't change."

Christian, our nation is in grave danger of going the way of Israel and Judah and suffering the **Woe** (the condition of deep suffering from misfortune, affliction, grief, ruinous calamity) of God Almighty. May God help us!

To read more of more related articles on the topic use the following links:

- America's Future – Dr. Charles Stanley, In Touch Ministries

07 – Let Us Reason Together

Background:

The Creator at Work

The Bible teaches that God is the great Creator of all that was, is and ever shall be. God created man "… in His own image." (Genesis 1:27). As such, God endowed man with a form of His own characteristics including the ability to reason. Christians believe that God's Word, The Holy Bible … and not human reasoning … is THE FINAL AUTHORITY regarding all matters of faith and human practice

God created man "in His Own image."

Though we are created in His image, God's reasoning is different from that of man. God's reasoning is unfathomable,

PERFECT, without flaw, always right (Job 11:7-8, Romans 11:33). God placed Adam and Eve in a perfect environment in the Garden of Eden with only one stipulation ... they were not to eat from the tree of the knowledge of good and evil (Genesis 2:16-17). But that wasn't enough for them. They believed the lie of Satan reasoning that if they ate of the tree they would "... be like God ..." (Genesis 3:5).

President Barack Obama and Vice President Joe Biden

In the face of today's political turmoil in the USA leading up to the November 2012 election, I am greatly concerned with the daily stream of untruthful rhetoric coming from so many of our national leaders and their supporters. The airways are filled with lies, attacks and political ads designed to pit the classes against each other ... all based on faulty reasoning. Why is it that so many of our leaders and potential leaders lean totally on their own understanding and reasoning without consulting God Almighty for His direction? In a word, the simple answer is because of "**SIN**."

Challenger's Mitt Romney and Paul Ryan

Because of man's sinfulness he often disagrees with God's reasoning and places himself above God violating the first of the Ten Commandments (Exodus 20:3). Blind ambition blocks and twists man's ability to reason. When politicians do not consult God about direction on important matters such as those affecting the future of our country, more often than not they make bad decisions. Through my sixty-nine years of observation, it is easy to conclude that many currently serving in the executive, legislative and judicial branches of the United States government have abandoned Godly reasoning altogether in favor of satisfying selfish motives ... and these motives are more often than not sinful.

Scripture: (all Scripture ESV (English Standard Version), unless otherwise noted)

Job 11:7-8 – *7 "Can you find out (fathom) the deep things of God? Can you find out the limit of the Almighty? 8 It is higher than heaven— what can you do? Deeper than Sheol—what can you know?*

Romans 11:33 – *Oh, the depth of the riches and wisdom and knowledge of God! How unsearchable are his judgments and how inscrutable his ways!*

Isaiah 1:16-18 – *[16] Wash yourselves; make yourselves clean; remove the evil of your deeds from before my eyes; cease to do evil, [17] learn to do good; seek justice, correct oppression; bring justice to the fatherless, plead the widow's cause. [18] "Come now, **let us reason together,** says the Lord: though your sins are like scarlet, they shall be as white as snow; though they are red like crimson, they shall become like wool."*

Isaiah 1:9-11 – *[9] If the Lord of hosts had not left us a few survivors, we should have been like Sodom, and become like Gomorrah. [10] Hear the word of the Lord, you rulers of Sodom! Give ear to the teaching of our God, you people of Gomorrah! [11] "What to me is the multitude of your sacrifices? says the Lord; I have had enough of burnt offerings of rams and the fat of well-fed beasts; I do not delight in the blood of bulls, or of lambs, or of goats.*

Acts 17:2 – *And Paul went in, as was his custom, and on three Sabbath days he reasoned with them from the Scriptures.*

Acts 17:11 – *Now these Jews were more noble than those in Thessalonica; they received the word with all eagerness, examining the Scriptures daily to see if these things were so.*

Acts 18:19 – *And they came to Ephesus, and he left them there, but he himself (Paul) went into the synagogue and reasoned with the Jews.*

1 Corinthians 6:12 – *"All things are lawful for me," but not all things are helpful. "All things are lawful for me," but I will not be dominated by anything.*

Discussion:

This article is not a scholarly attempt to provide a full discourse on reasoning. Rather, it is an attempt to shed light on how human reasoning without the inspiration of God and His reasoning can easily be faulty.

Since I refer so often to "reason" and "reasoning" throughout this article, here's how Webster defines **"reason": the power of comprehending, inferring, or thinking especially in orderly rational ways.**

I realize that many well-known writers have penned a multitude of articles and on what is involved in "reasoning." Thomas Paine published his still famous and widely distributed book promoting deism, "The Age of Reason", in three parts in 1794, 1795 and 1807. Deism called for "free rational inquiry" and rejected some of the important tenets of the Bible such as the miracles and the Bible's teaching that there was only "one true faith". As for me Paine was/is absolutely wrong on both of these points. Regardless of man's position, depending on man's reasoning ability to interpret scripture is an attempt to put man on God's level and most assuredly is not possible.

God invites man to reason with Him. Reasoning with God requires that man respect God's position and His far superior perfect knowledge. Man must reason with God on His terms. Doing the opposite or leaving God out of our reasoning altogether is a guarantee for disaster. Isaiah the prophet recorded the words of the Lord in Isaiah 1:18, *"Come now, let us reason together, says the Lord..."* as he promised that our scarlet sins would become like wool (white, cleaned, forgiven). Of course, this requires that we accept the Lord Jesus as our personal Savior (see How to Become a Christian).

Isaiah lived in the eighth century B.C. during the resurgence of Assyria as a major power. He prophesied in Jerusalem in particular to King Ahaz (Israel) and King Hezekiah (Judah) and two other kings. Many of his prophesies spoke directly to the political situation during Isaiah's lifetime. Isaiah reminded them of how God destroyed Sodom and Gomorrah because of their wickedness (Isaiah 1:9-11). Isaiah knew that Israel and Judah were headed down the wrong path as each shunned God and placed their faith in human leadership ... leadership that reasoned that alliances with ungodly nations such as Egypt would protect them from the overwhelming strength of Assyria. Both Israel and Judah continued to depend upon their own reasoning and each fell into captivity of their enemies. Could the USA be any different?

Let's bring in a common example of faulty human reasoning. Have you or one of your children been personally involved in a conversation such as this: "Oh, it won't hurt you to try this just once!" What a trap authored by Satan! Too many teenagers are unwittingly dragged into a life of drug abuse by swallowing this line of reasoning. If your friends are doing what is wrong in the sight of God, then my advice is to dump them and stay out of situations to begin with that will compromise your faith and your reasoning. My wife and I taught our son early on that he should never put himself into the position of being too embarrassed to say no when his peers were trying to drag him into their sin.

The ability to reason is a gift from God. Much of learning in areas such as science, mathematics, technology, engineering, information and computation systems, accounting, actuarial science, statistics, rocket science, etc., requires a significant human ability to reason. God created us to reason. My entire business life required intensive reasoning and I am thankful for God's gift. How dull would it be to live a robotic life without the ability to reason? As Christians we are to strive to be more like God with every ounce of our energy. Unfortunately, our sinfulness is constantly in the way of accomplishing that goal.

After Paul met Jesus on the road to Damascus and left his life as a Pharisee bent on punishing and even killing Christians, he became a fervent disciple for the Lord spreading the message of salvation through Jesus Christ on multiple missionary journeys. Paul often reasoned in the Jewish synagogues with the religious leaders (Acts 17:2, Acts 17:11) to advance the cause of Christ.

Reflection:

Let me give some pictorial examples of how twentieth century leadership's evil and twisted reasoning ran amuck with disastrous human consequences. How many can you name? Answers are presented below at the end of the article.

I think that we all can agree that man's reasoning can lead to disastrous tragedy. A tyrannical German leader coerced an entire nation to blindly follow man's reasoning resulting in World War II and causing the death of millions upon millions of innocent people and leaving millions of children dead or orphaned. A perverted religious leader led 909 of his deceived followers to commit what the leader called "revolutionary suicide". The total included over 200 murdered children. What an outrage! A Chinese Communist leader massacred an estimated 40-70 million people in the name of The People's Revolution. The Supreme Court of the USA decided that the aborting of unborn children was constitutional resulting in the senseless murder of 53 million babies through legal abortions through 2011.

Two current examples of man's ridiculous reasoning in direct conflict with the teachings of Almighty God and His perfect reasoning are abortion and same-sex marriage (see On Child Sacrifice, On the Sanctity of Life and Abortion, Lifestyle Choices and Biblical Truth, The Sanctity of Marriage.) Each human life, born or unborn is precious to God. He creates each one In His Own Image. How can we stand by and so callously allow the murder of our children? The Bible clearly defines marriage as being between a man and a woman, not a man and a man, nor a woman and a woman. How can so many reason that same-sex marriage is right when God specifically forbids it?

Godly human reasoning doesn't mean compromising the Word or your Faith ... it is quite the opposite. Godly human reasoning supports the Word and your Faith. I completely agree with Christian author Don Stewart featured in the Blue Letter Bible when he states: "The Bible is not against reasoning. To the contrary Scripture encourages people to reason. What the Bible is against is unaided human reason that attempts to judge Scripture. Reason must always submit itself to the truth of God's Word. This is the way that God intended it to be. "

My favorite religious leader is evangelist Dr. Billy Graham. As of the time of the writing this article he is 93 years old being born on November 7, 1918. Dr. Graham is mostly confined to his home in North Carolina due to his failing health. Yet, Dr. Graham continues to regularly communicate through his prayer letter with the outside world about God and His forgiveness through His son Jesus Christ. Here's an excerpt from his July 24, 2012 article – My Heart Aches for America:

> "Just a few weeks ago in a prominent city in the South, Christian chaplains who serve the police department were ordered to no longer mention the Name of Jesus in prayer. It was reported that during a recent police-sponsored event, the only person allowed to pray was someone who addressed "the being in the room." Similar scenarios are now commonplace in towns across America. Our society strives to avoid any possibility of offending anyone—except God.

Yet the farther we get from God, the more the world spirals out of control.

My heart aches for America and its deceived people. The wonderful news is that our Lord is a God of mercy, and He responds to repentance. In Jonah's day, Nineveh was the lone world superpower - wealthy, unconcerned, and self-centered. When the Prophet Jonah finally traveled to Nineveh and proclaimed God's warning, people heard and repented."

Like Dr. Graham, my heart aches and is so burdened with the message of this article. America is just like Israel and Judah. Our leaders continually depend upon their own reasoning without regard to God's Word. Preachers preach. Listeners listen. Nothing happens. How long will God put up with us? How deep does our nation have to sink before God has had enough? Who will stand on the Lord's side and be counted.

In 1 Corinthians 6:12 Paul said *"All things are lawful unto me, but all things are not expedient: all things are lawful for me, but I will not be brought under the control of any."* Joshua emphasized that people must make their own choices. *"And if it is evil in your eyes to serve the Lord, choose this day whom you will serve, whether the gods your fathers served in the region beyond the River, or the gods of the Amorites in whose land you dwell. But as for me and my house, we will serve the Lord"* (Joshua 24:15).

My prayer is that one by one we will realize what a mess we are in and turn away from our sinful ways. Pray for our leaders to turn their lives over to the Lord Jesus Christ. Carefully consider your vote in the November 2012 election. Vote your convictions, but make sure your convictions line up with God's reasoning.

One final admonishment from God's Word: Proverbs 14:12 - *There is a way that seems right to a man, but its end is the way of death.* **May God help us!!**

20th Century Twisted Reasoning Leaders

Click on the links to explore more information:

1. *Mao Tse Tung* – *Chinese Communist Revolutionary*
2. *Idi Amin* – *Military Dictator of Uganda*
3. *Adolf Hitler* – *Dictator of Nazi Germany*
4. *Saddam Hussein* – *President of Iraq*
5. *Fidel Castro* – *President of Cuba and First Secretary of the Communist Party*
6. *Jim Jones* – *Founder and Leader of the Peoples Temple – Jonestown*
7. *David Koresh* – *Branch Davidian religious sect*
8. *Osama Bin Laden* – *founder of al-Qaeda*
9. *Kim Jon Il* – *Supreme Leader of North Korea*

08 – In His Time

Background:

I have always known that I am a very impatient man. I think I was born that way. As a child I never wanted to wait for anything. I remember the anxiety and impatience I had as eight year old boy because I had to wait another year for my first bicycle since Santa "didn't have room on his sleigh" that year. Those closest to me, including my parents, my wife, our son and my siblings know very well of my impatience and have rightfully told me about it so many times over the years.

The vocational work that I performed for over forty-five years in the Information Technology field was stressful and built around deadlines and often resulted in severe penalties when those deadlines were not met. So my profession fit well with my type "A" personality. As a leader, I required those on my project teams to set goals, determine specific and real requirements, develop and stick to realistic timelines, complete the effort in the agreed upon time-frame, and then develop lessons learned to improve the quality of the next project. I must admit that I sometimes thought of myself as a person who could make things happen ... someone with a special ability to deliver as agreed upon and in the time-frame promised.

Looking back on my life now, I expected just about everything to happen **"in my time"**, not just the work related projects, but just about everything in my personal life as well. Over the past eighteen months as I have dealt with significant health issues for the first time in my life. I have come to realize that my view of time and God's view of time don't always line up very well. I want these medical issues to be behind me, but they continue and have impacted me in such a way that I now faithfully realize that they are in God's hands and He will deal with them **"in His time."**

As a younger man I often prayed that God would give me wisdom and patience. Most of those prayers were genuinely earnest. But some were prayed with deep set reservations and even sometimes in a selfish demanding manner similar to the comical prayer that goes something like: "Lord, please give me patience ... and give it to me right now!"

This brings me to the point of this article ... namely; God alone is in control of time!!! Time is His. He does things "in His time." God was there before time was established. God was there at creation and He created everything "in His time." God was there when He led the Amorite Abraham away from His home in Ur to the place God chose "in His time." God was there when He led his chosen children out of Egypt into the promised-land "in His time." God was there when David killed Goliath and when he was crowned King of Israel "in His time. God was there when He allowed Israel and Judah's enemies to devastate their homeland, kill their mighty warriors and force most of those remaining alive into bondage "in His time." God was there when He sent Jesus to be born of a non-descript virgin girl 'in His time." God was there when Jesus was crucified "in His time." God was there when Jesus was raised from the dead and conquered sin and death once and for all "in His time. God was there when Jesus ascended back into Heaven "in His time." God has promised that Jesus will again return to this earth to claim His chosen ones "in His time." I'm sure you get the point!

Scripture:

Ecclesiastes 3:1-11 (KJV) – focus on verse 11.

*[1]To every thing there is a season, and a time to every purpose under the heaven: [2]A time to be born, and a time to die; a time to plant, and a time to pluck up that which is planted; [3]A time to kill, and a time to heal; a time to break down, and a time to build up; [4]A time to weep, and a time to laugh; a time to mourn, and a time to dance; [5]A time to cast away stones, and a time to gather stones together; a time to embrace, and a time to refrain from embracing; [6]A time to get, and a time to lose; a time to keep, and a time to cast away; [7]A time to rend, and a time to sew; a time to keep silence, and a time to speak; [8]A time to love, and a time to hate; a time of war, and a time of peace. [9]What profit hath he that worketh in that wherein he laboureth? [10]I have seen the travail, which God hath given to the sons of men to be exercised in it. [11]**He hath made every thing beautiful in his time:** also he hath set the world in their heart, so that no man can find out the work that God maketh from the beginning to the end.*

Discussion:

The above scripture passage comes from the Book of Ecclesiastes. The Chronological Study Bible (TCSB) of The New King James Version of the Bible published by Thomas Nelson describes Ecclesiastes as a "bleak and weary" book focused on the inability of man to understand the inexplicable mysteries of life. The overall thesis, "...All is vanity" (Ecc. 1:2) permeates the entire book. At the very end of the book, the Preacher finally seems "to make peace with his world and his God" (Ecc. 12:13-14 NASB): *[13] The conclusion, when all has been heard, is: fear God and keep His commandments, because this applies to every person. [14] For God will bring every act to judgment, everything which is hidden, whether it is good or evil.*

But there is really a scriptural gem found in Ecclesiastes 3:11 (KJV) – "*11 He hath made every thing beautiful in his time: also he hath set the world in their heart, so that no man can find out the work that God maketh from the beginning to the end.*" I like the translation for the last part of verse 11 as presented in the NIV: *11 He has made everything beautiful in its time. He has also set eternity in the human heart; yet no one can fathom what God has done from beginning to end.* Why should I expect things to happen in my time? My time may be the wrong time. Only God knows the right time! When things happen "in His (God's) time" *every thing is beautiful.* Who am I to think that I know when it is best for things to happen? God ordained time. He, and He alone, is in control of time. Who am I to think that I have the human ability to reason beyond God's instruction in the Bible to **"fathom"** what God has done, is doing, and will do to accomplish His ultimate purpose. God wrote our life instruction manual, the Bible. It is His perfect and infallible Word. It is without error. Nothing ever happens in His time early or late. It is always in accordance with what is "in His time." He's an on-time God! Every time!!

Reflection:

I am encouraged by my recent medical hardships to allow God to also be the God of all comfort for me personally and to my friends and Christian brothers and sisters. Paul said to those new Christian converts in the city of Corinth in 2 Corinthians 1:3 (NIV) – *"Praise be to the God and Father of our Lord Jesus Christ, the Father of compassion and the God of all comfort, 4 who comforts us in all our troubles, so that we can comfort those in any trouble with the comfort we ourselves receive from God."* I will look to Him in His time, and to Him alone, for that deep comfort, the inner healing and the encouragement to continue my earthly life journey and share

God's message with as many as I can before I join those already in eternity.

Paul also encouraged the church at Phillipi saying *"I have learned to be content whatever the circumstances. I know what it is to be in need and I know what it is to have plenty. I have learned the secret of being content in any and every situation, whether well fed or hungry, whether living in plenty or in want. I can do everything through him who gives me strength."* (Philippians 4:11-13) NIV.

Are you as hard-headed as I am? Are you listening to the plain word of God? The children of Israel didn't. In their own time they allowed the worship of other gods such as Baal to replace the worship of the one and only true Jehovah God. In the midst of their wayward lives, God's prophet Jeremiah using God's own words continually reminded Israel that they had repeatedly taken things into their own hands: *"While you were doing all these things, declares the Lord, I spoke to you again and again, but you did not listen; I called you but you did not answer"* (Jeremiah 7:13 NIV).

God said through Paul in Galatians 4:4-7 (NIV) that He sent his son Jesus into the world to pay the price for man's sin when the time was right. It was "in His time." *"⁴ But when the set time had fully come, God sent his Son, born of a woman, born under the law, ⁵ to redeem those under the law, that we might receive adoption to sonship. ⁶ Because you are his sons, God sent the Spirit of his Son into our hearts, the Spirit who calls out, "Abba, and Father." ⁷ So you are no longer a slave, but God's child; and since you are his child, God has made you also an heir."*

I find this verse particularly comforting in my recent stressful times: Psalm 69:13 (NIV) – *"But I pray to you, Lord, in the time of Your favor; in Your great love, O God, answer me with Your sure salvation.* " But at the same time, I realize that God has a purpose in my mortal travail and that "in His time" and when I humble myself, that only He has the strong and mighty hand to lift me up. Peter spoke to this as well in 1 Peter 5:6 (NIV) when he said *"Humble Yourselves, therefore, under God's mighty hand, that he may lift you up in due time."*

The Maranatha Singers have recorded a wonderful version of a song written by Diane Ball in 1978. The lyrics are provided below and are the property of Maranatha! Music. This is one of those songs like "Thank You Lord for Saving My Soul" that will keep running through your mind over and over once you hear it. I was exposed to it many years ago, but it has recently come back to my mind and I could not get past the message.

In His Time

In His time, in His time
He makes all things beautiful in His time
Lord, please show me every day
As You're teaching me Your way
And I'll do just what You say
In Your time.

In Your time, in Your time
You make all things beautiful in Your time
Lord, my life to You I bring
May each song I have to sing
Be to You a lovely thing
In Your time

Be to You a lovely thing
In Your time.

I can't think of a more fitting way to end this article than for you to view a couple of videos of this song by going to these YouTube links. Both will allow you to sing or hum along.

Video one with beautiful scenes of God's nature set to the music with lyrics.

In His Time - Maranatha! Singers - Video One

Video two with scripture and lyrics:

In His Time - Video Two

09 – When God Has Had Enough

Background:

There are consequences for ignoring the commands of God. God is forgiving, but at the same time, God is righteous. He cannot and will not ignore man's sin. Sin has eternal consequences. Additionally, man, both individually and collectively, often suffers here on earth as a result of sin. This has been true since the beginning of time. Consider the consequences of the sin of Adam and Eve and the guilt placed on all future generations.

The same is true of nations. Even the highly favored and blessed nation of Israel formed by God through the descendants of Jacob suffered earthly consequences for their sin and for continuing to turn their back on Jehovah God. Having possessed the Promised Land through God's mighty power, they shamelessly ignored His commands and even worshiped other gods. Among others, God hand-picked Amos and Hosea often referred to as Minor Prophets, to deliver His message of the impending doom for the northern kingdom of Israel. The consequences of their sinful ways and their worship of foreign gods would lead them to a massive slaughter and a century's long captivity. Ultimately, the southern kingdom of Judah would also fall to the Babylonians as foretold by the prophet Jeremiah. Judah too would be torn away from their homes only to live in exile for several generations at a later date.

Scripture: All scripture references are taken from "The Chronological Study Bible" (TCSB), copyright 1997 by Thomas Nelson, Inc. unless otherwise noted.

Amos 2:4 – *Thus says the Lord: "For three transgressions of Judah, and for four, I will not turn away its punishment, because they have despised the law of the Lord, and have not kept His commandments. Their lies lead them astray, lies which their fathers followed."*

Amos 2:6 – *Thus says the Lord: "For three transgressions of Israel, and for four, I will not turn away punishment ... "*

Amos 7:11 – *For thus Amos has said: Jeroboam shall die by the sword, And Israel shall surely be led away captive from their own land."*

Hosea 1: 2-4 – *When the Lord began to speak to Hosea, the Lord said to Hosea: "Go take yourself a wife of harlotry, for the land has committed great harlotry by departing from the Lord." So he went and took Gomer the daughter of Diblaim, and she conceived and bore him a son. Then the Lord said to him: "Call his name Jezreel, for in a little while I will avenge the bloodshed of Jezreel on the house of Jehu, and **bring an end to the kingdom of the house of Israel.**"*

Discussion:

Amos was one of the Minor Prophets and not the only one to severely chide Israel for their complacency regarding God's commands. Amos was from Judah, but he primarily spoke to Israel. He foretold of God's judgment that would surely come. The ministry of Amos occurred before 753 B.C. He was a sheep herder from Tekoa in Judah during the reign of king Uzziah. At the same time Jeroboam II, the son of Joash, was the king of Israel. Amos, chapters 1-2, records that God sent a vision to Amos regarding the transgressions and impending judgment for the surrounding nations of Damascus, Gaza,

Tyre, Edom and Ammon. This would have been music to the ears of Judah and Israel.

But God and Amos did not stop there. God also pronounced to Amos harsh judgment for His chosen people, both Israel and Judah. In particular, Israel's pride had swelled during Amos' time because of their relatively minor military victories over Judah's Lo Debar and Karnaim by their "*own strength*" (Amos 6:13). Worst of all, Israel had continued to worship false gods. Israel had been called to be God's special people and to worship Yahweh alone. God pronounced the destruction, slaughter and exile of Israel in Amos 9:8 – *"Behold, the eyes of the Lord God are on the sinful kingdom, And I will destroy it from the face of the earth…"*

Hosea was native to the northern kingdom of Israel. Hosea spoke against the worship of false gods such as Baal and Asherah. These were religions that promoted the worst kind of sexual behavior in their worship including prostitution, or as referred to by Hosea, harlotry. Hosea had first-hand experience with that in his own family (see chapter one of Hosea). He passionately pleaded with the unfaithful bride of God, Israel, to return from their harlotry or face the consequences. Hosea foresees the fall, but he also sees and predicts Israel's restoration when they ultimately return to God.

Just as God had so easily brought His children into the Promised Land, He removed them from that land and scattered them throughout the world.

Reflection:

God will not be mocked. There are consequences to sin, both here and now and for eternity. God's righteousness demands it. Could the same consequences God allowed to fall on Israel and Judah be true for America? Could we be at the point in our history **"when God has had enough?"** I for one believe that we are wearing God's patience very, very thin. When one, or a nation, continues to live in sin, never accepting God's plan for forgiveness of sin, the eternal consequences are sad and dire. But God does provide a way out of our dilemma. He has provided His Son Jesus Christ as the deliverer from the consequences of our sin. Americans need to turn to Jesus for salvation. America must stand for what is right in the sight of God. I pray that it is not too late for us.

God has promised us that He will heal our land. But there are requirements. God said *"If my people who are called by My name will humble themselves, and pray and seek My face, and turn from their wicked ways, then I will hear from heaven, and will forgive their sin and heal their land."* (2 Chronicles 7:14 – NKJV)

Christian, it is time that we take action and stand up to the world around us. There is a price that the nations will pay for willful disobedience of God's commands and the sinful worship of other gods. Together we can make a difference. Be bold in your witness and make His message known.

Oh, Heavenly Father, may I never be ashamed of my faith in You and have the courage to stand up and speak up for what is right in the sight of God!

10 – The Sanctity of Marriage

Background:

Jim and Charlotte Davenport
April 7, 2012 at our Granddaughter's Wedding

In August 2012 my wife and I will have been married for forty-nine years. ALL of the years have been God blessed. We met at a church sponsored summer youth camp in the north Georgia Mountains when I was a rising senior in high school. I was immediately struck with her personal beauty, her purity, her character, and perhaps most importantly, her Christian behavior. She was different that the other girls that I had dated. I wanted to ask her out but the timing just wasn't right. Truthfully, she didn't care much for me in the beginning. I later learned that some of her girlfriends had told her that I had the reputation of dating a lot of girls then dropping them. In other words, I wouldn't be a good match for her … period.

Months later I asked her to come to one of my basketball games. To my delight, she came. I was thrilled. Over time I won her over and she was my date at my Senior Prom. By that time I knew that I wanted to partner with her for a lifetime. In my eyes she would be a perfect mate. We dated no one else after we began dating. A little over two years later and after my sophomore year in college we were married. Ultimately I completed college and graduate school with her strong help.

I know that God put us together. There has never been a doubt in my mind. God blessed us with a wonderful son. We raised him in a Christian home. God led him to marry a wonderful Christian young woman and they too have raised their children in a Christian home. His daughter recently completed college and married a fine Christian young man and we fully expect them to live a successful Christian life led by the Lord. Our grandson just graduated from high school with honors. He is bound for college and is dating a fine Christian young lady. We fully expect him to lead a successful Christian life as well.

God has blessed us in so many ways spiritually and physically. I could not imagine sharing my life with anyone else. God put us together. He knew what was best for us. There are dozens of scripture passages that speak to the sanctity of marriage. Let's examine my favorites for the purpose of this article.

Scripture: (All English Standard Version – ESV – unless otherwise noted)

(1) Genesis 2:18 – *Then the Lord God said, "It is not good that the man should be alone; I will make him a helper fit for him."*

(2) Genesis 2:24 – *Therefore a man shall leave his father and his mother and hold fast to his wife, and they shall become one flesh.*

(3) Matthew 19:4-6 – *He answered, "Have you not read that he who created them from the beginning made them male and female, and said, 'Therefore a man shall leave his father and his mother and hold fast to his wife, and the two shall become one flesh'? So they are no longer two but one flesh. What therefore God has joined together, let not man separate."*

1 Corinthians 7:39 – *A wife is bound to her husband as long as he lives. But if her husband dies, she is free to be married to whom she wishes, only in the Lord.*

(4) Proverbs 18:22 – *He who finds a wife finds a good thing and obtains favor from the Lord.*

(5) Hebrews 13:4 – Let marriage be held in honor among all, and let the marriage bed be undefiled, for God will judge the sexually immoral and adulterous.

(6) Exodus 20:14 – You shall not commit adultery.

(7) Luke 16:18 – *Everyone who divorces his wife and marries commits adultery, and he who marries a woman divorced from her husband commits adultery.*

(8) 1 Corinthians 7:1-5 – *Now concerning the matters about which you wrote: "It is good for a man not to have sexual relations with a woman." But because of the temptation to sexual immorality, each man should have his own wife and each woman her own husband. The husband should give to his wife her conjugal rights, and likewise the wife to her husband. For the wife does not have authority over her own body, but the husband does. Likewise the husband does not have authority over his own body, but the wife does. Do not deprive one another, except perhaps by agreement for a limited time, that you may devote yourselves to prayer; but then come*

together again, so that Satan may not tempt you because of your lack of self-control.

(9) Mark 10:2-7 – *And Pharisees came up and in order to test him asked, "Is it lawful for a man to divorce his wife?" He answered them, "What did Moses command you?" They said, "Moses allowed a man to write a certificate of divorce and to send her away." And Jesus said to them, "Because of your hardness of heart he wrote you this commandment. But from the beginning of creation, 'God made them male and female. Therefore a man shall leave his father and mother and hold fast to his wife, and the two shall become one flesh.' So they are no longer two but one flesh. What therefore God has joined together let not man separate."*

(10) Matthew 5:31-32 – *"It has been said, 'Anyone who divorces his wife must give her a certificate of divorce. But I tell you that anyone who divorces his wife, except for sexual immorality, causes her to become an adulteress, and anyone who marries the divorced woman commits adultery."*

Discussion:

Webster defines **"sanctity"** as follows: 1 – holiness of life and character; godliness. 2 – the quality or state of being holy or sacred; inviolability (refers to being secure from violation or profanation.) Thus the phrase "sanctity of marriage" refers to marriage as being sacred, holy, secure from violation, and of God.

I don't believe that my selected verses need that much discussion for the purpose of this article. These words are not only time-honored and such sensible advice; they are direct communications from God Almighty himself recorded in His Holy Word. Those that believe in Jehovah God and do their best to follow His commands understand that ALL of the Bible is true, inerrant (without error), and is THE GUIDE for our how we as His children are to conduct our lives and our marriage.

So here's a brief synopsis of the selected verses. Marriage was ordained by God (1, 2) to be between a man and a woman. Marriage is designed by God to be permanent (3). Those who are married find God's favor (4). Marriage is to be honorable and God judges sexual immorality and adultery in a marriage (5, 6, 7). The husband and wife are to yield authority over their bodies to each other (8). God does not expect or want a married couple to divorce (9), but allows it when adultery is present (10).

Unfortunately the wonderful and blessed marriage my wife and I have experienced is not that experienced by today's average American male/female couple. The majority (52% according to recent government statistics) of today's male/female "couples" are not married. They just "live" together as though they were married, at least for a season, and sometimes then get married. Often times when things aren't going well enough to suit one of the partners, they just leave ... only to start another relationship where the partners live together. Many argue this is a way to avoid divorce and that it gives the couple time to learn about each other BEFORE they make a permanent marriage commitment. Life is full of excuses for why people don't follow God's commands.

Sadly, co-habitation has been "sold" to the American public as an acceptable alternative to traditional marriage. It has been plastered on our TV screens and the subject of countless Hollywood productions. Even many Christians have been deceived by all of the hype and they too participate in this lifestyle. This is a very dangerous practice and goes directly against what God has taught us through His Word, the Bible. The Bible is clear: co-habitation without marriage is sin and sin has earthly consequences. (See my recent article: Sin's Earthly Consequences)

A Gallup poll conducted just prior to Christmas in 2009 found that 78% of Americans identified themselves as "Christian." I find it strange that 52% of male/female couples in the United States are living together, unmarried. Coincidentally, 52% of Americans now favor "same-sex marriage." Such marriages are in direct violation of God's Word, no matter how much you try to argue otherwise. By the way, having to refer to a "couple" as "male/female" in and of itself bothers me.

So, man has once again overstepped his authority and placed himself above God. The Jews did this many times and always suffered the consequences. I am reminded of when Moses was on Mount Sinai receiving The Ten Commandments and the people took things into their own hands. When Moses descended from the mountain he found the people had fashioned a golden calf so they could worship this god like others were doing in Egypt and other countries. Such disobedience caused their emerging nation tremendous pain and agony as they wandered in the desert for forty years before finally entering the promised land.

Later in the history of God's people, one king after another in Israel and Judah **did not do what was right in the sight of the Lord.** Instead they adopted the ungodly and immoral practices of their neighboring countries and worshiped other gods such as Baal, Ashtoreth and Molech. They even participated in perverted sexual orgies as part of their pagan worship. Does this sound familiar? It does to me. Israel and Judah ultimately paid a staggering price for their sin. They suffered the slaughter of hundreds of thousands of their mighty men (soldiers) and citizens resulting in the complete collapse of their nation. They lost their homeland. They lost their way of life. They lost touch with Almighty God. And as a result, they spent generation after generation in captivity in a foreign and cruel land.

Reflection:

Let me take a short side-trip here to provide some insight into a related topic and America's current political and spiritual situation. Acceptance of the gay lifestyle by Americans is now in the majority. Perhaps this is the REAL reason that President Obama recently came out with his full-fledged support for same-sex marriage. President Obama has actually voiced three differing stances on this issue over the past four years and will likely change again after the election. Each change of heart the President has voiced has coincided with that which was politically expedient at the time. His positions are in direct opposition to what the Bible teaches. I can only presume that the President has placed his beliefs above those of Almighty God. Why? So he can garner enough votes to get re-elected. That's why! One has to conclude that the President's recent choice to support same-sex marriage is strictly for political reasons. Why else would he go against the Christian "majority," the 78%, at this point in time? His advisers have assured him that he will receive more votes by taking this position. I'm rather sure his advisers are right unless Christians, including the 78% who claim to be Christians, stand up for what God expects of them.

Take a look at excerpts from an article that recently appeared in the New York Times ... yes, the liberal New York Times. Click on this link: Gay Marriage Rally It is no secret that I am an ultra-conservative by national news media standards. I am a Bible believing Baptist that lives in a southern state. What our President is advocating, same-sex marriage, is an abomination according to the scripture (Leviticus 18:22 – *"Thou shalt not lie with mankind, as with womankind: it is an abomination."*) No one, especially a Christian ... and including President Obama ... can alter God's viewpoint nor choose to ignore it. There is just no other Godly way homosexuality and same-sex marriage can be viewed. It is a sin and not to be practiced. Our leadership, our nation and future generations will suffer immeasurably and pay the consequences for our nation's potential agreement with such an unGodly position. America is in a downward, satanic moral spiral. We are sick and need healing.

Interestingly, since the announcement of support by the President, the NAACP has also come out in support of same-sex marriage. I'm not at all surprised by that move. However, I am agonizingly surprised that many minority pastors are also falling in line and supporting the NAACP and President Obama's position as a civil rights issue. Come on! I don't see how any pastor of a Christian church can realistically ignore the Bible's teachings about marriage. How can so many pastors rationalize this position and compromise their pulpit by supporting a practice that is absolutely condemned by the Bible. I will have to leave the ultimate decision to you. But for me, it is all about supporting President Obama... their preferred political candidate. No matter what is right in the sight of God and no matter what the Bible says. How sad! I suppose I could be branded as a racist because I have "negatively" mentioned the NAACP. So be it! I know my heart.

I expect to receive some negative feedback on this article. I usually do when I write on controversial subjects with the Bible as my guide. That's okay with me. You see, I am on the Lord's side. I believe in the Lord's Word. Love, morality, truth, sin and justice are all defined by God ... not man.

Marriage is holy. Marriage is of God. Marriage is between a man and a woman, not a man and a man, and not a woman and a woman. I believe wholly in the Sanctity of Marriage!

11 – Sin's Earthly Consequences

Background:

In a previous article I raised the point that sin has both earthly and eternal consequences (see <u>When God Has Had Enough</u>). While the blood of Jesus was shed for the forgiveness of sin and accepting Him as our Savior guarantees an eternal sinless life in Heaven with Him, we often pay the consequences for our sin on earth while we are here.

There is a portion of the scripture that came to mind when I thought this topic through. It deals with King Uzziah of Judah and takes place almost 2,800 years ago. I have been reading and studying *Thomas Nelson's New King James Version of The Chronological Study Bible* (NKJV-TCSB) over the past couple of years. Reading the Bible chronologically has significantly enhanced my understanding of the Old Testament. The Bible is presented in chronological order regardless of the usual book/chapter/verse structure. I'm certainly no Bible scholar. All I know is what the Holy Spirit has interpreted to me through what I read and have been taught by my local church since I was a child. But this one thing I know for sure. Sin has consequences … even for the best of God's children.

Scripture:

2 Chronicles 26 – all verses in this article from the NKJV unless otherwise noted.

*¹Now all the people of Judah took Uzziah, who was sixteen years old, and made him king instead of his father Amaziah. … ³ Uzziah was sixteen years old when he became king, and he reigned fifty-two years in Jerusalem. His mother's name was Jecholiah of Jerusalem. ⁴ **And he did what was right in the*** *sight of the Lord, according to all that his father Amaziah had done. [5] He sought God in the days of Zechariah, who had understanding in the visions of God; and as long as he sought the Lord, God made him prosper. ... [16] But when he was strong his heart was lifted up, to his destruction, for he transgressed against the Lord his God by entering the temple of the Lord to burn incense on the altar of incense. [17] So Azariah the priest went in after him, and with him were eighty priests of the Lord—valiant men. [18] And they withstood King Uzziah, and said to him, "It is not for you, Uzziah, to burn incense to the Lord, but for the priests, the sons of Aaron, who are consecrated to burn incense. Get out of the sanctuary, for you have trespassed! You shall have no honor from the Lord God."* ... *[19] Then Uzziah became furious; and he had a censer in his hand to burn incense. And while he was angry with the priests, leprosy broke out on his forehead, before the priests in the house of the Lord, beside the incense altar. [20] And Azariah the chief priest and all the priests looked at him, and there, on his forehead, he was leprous; so they thrust him out of that place. Indeed he also hurried to get out, because the Lord had struck him. [21] King Uzziah was a leper until the day of his death. He dwelt in an isolated house, because he was a leper; for he was cut off from the house of the Lord. Then Jotham his son was over the king's house, judging the people of the land.*

Discussion:

King Uzziah was a great ruler by most any measure. Over his fifty-two years (793-753 BC) on the throne of the southern kingdom of Judah, he led the nation to great political success, expansion and prosperity. The Bible says that this was as a result of Uzziah **doing what was right in the sight of God**. Uzziah was sixteen years old when he was placed on the throne by all the people of Judah. According to 2 Chronicles

26:2, his father Amaziah also **did what was right in the sight of God**.

But Uzziah violated the role of God's political leader by taking over a priestly responsibility when he burned incense in the innermost part of the Temple. This was against the priests will and they tried to stop him. More importantly, this also violated God's will. The Law of Moses required that the priests were the only ones that could perform the ritual of sacrifices (Numbers 3:5-10). Entering the interior part of the Temple was forbidden to all except for certain orders of Levitical priests. Therefore, the King of Judah was forbidden to enter the interior of the Temple.

It was common practice in that day for the kings of neighboring political entities to offer sacrifices to their gods. The kings of these other nations were not only the head of the nation; they often had the status as a high priest with special privileges. Sometimes the king was even thought of as a god himself, and he declared himself such. Consider the Egyptian kings … they were considered to be gods embodied in a man.

In burning incense in the innermost part of the Temple, Uzziah was acting like his peers, the kings of other nations. Those peers were not only the political leader, they were also expected to be the religious leader and high priest and offer incense to their pagan gods. Uzziah sinned by violating God's Mosaic command. As a result, God immediately struck Uzziah with leprosy and he lived out the rest of his life in solitude.

While the southern kingdom prospered greatly under Uzziah's leadership, the northern kingdom was in chaos as one king after another was assassinated (the northern kingdom of Israel ultimately fell to the Assyrians in 722 BC). The Bible says that Uzziah **"did what was right in the sight of the Lord** (2

Chronicles 26:4)." Nevertheless, as a consequence of his sin, Uzziah suffered from leprosy, misery and isolation for the last ten years of his life.

Uzziah's twenty-five year old son, Jotham, served as co-regent for those last and miserable years of Uzziah's life and for six more years after Uzziah's passing. Both father and son **did what was right in the sight of the Lord** for most things and the prosperity of the southern kingdom flourished. However, Jotham's son Ahaz did not follow his father's ways and the scripture records that he "**did not do what was right in the sight of the Lord** (2 Kings 16:2)." Let's save discussion on that for another day.

Reflection:

But Dad (and/or Mom) ... "Everyone else is doing it!" I bet you have heard that before! I can remember saying it to my parents. And I can remember our son saying that to us when he was a teenager. That is certainly not a reason to defy God's commands. There are consequences to sin here on earth. Matthew 7:13-14 says *"13 Enter ye in at the strait gate: for wide is the gate, and broad is the way, that leadeth to destruction, and many there be which go in thereat: 14 Because strait is the gate, and narrow is the way, which leadeth unto life, and few there be that find it."*

What about you? Have you done "**what is right in the sight of the Lord**?" All of us are sinners and have fallen short of the glory of God. The point is, there are consequences for our sin ... both here on earth and for an eternity. Jesus died for our sins ... ALL of them. Only by accepting Jesus as Savior can we be forgiven of ALL of our sins and spend an eternity with God in Heaven. If you have not done so, please visit this link to learn how you too can become a Christian. <u>How To Become A Christian</u>

And Christian, don't expect to avoid the consequences of your sin on earth. How many Christian families are broken every year by unfaithfulness? Sadly, many Christians do now feel they should suffer the consequences of their sin here on earth. But friends, the Bible speaks plainly and truthfully about this throughout its pages. As Christians, we should stay in a constant state of conviction and confession, reminded of the fact that God has prepared a way of escape from our sinful life. The prize is eternity with Him in Heaven!

Here's a link to a song recorded by The Good News in 1990 from their southern gospel album *Jesus Will Lead Me*. The title of the song is "Sin Will Take You Farther." The first two lines of the song are "Sin will take you farther than you want to go. Slowly, but wholly, taking control." Oh, how true that is!!

<u>Sin Will Take You Farther</u>

12 – God's Glory Roll

Background:

I have been thinking about the love of God a lot lately and how He cares so for His children. I've been thinking about Heaven too and how God has reserved a special place just for me because I am one of his saved children.

I became a Christian when I was twelve years old when our church was having a revival. I remember it like it was yesterday. My Sunday School teacher was the elderly Mr. Meek. Actually one of the things I remember about Mr. Meek is that he was a terrible communicator ... especially to twelve year old boys. He stumbled through every lesson ... week after week. Twelve year old boys, and there were about ten of us in his class at the time, are rambunctious and the last thing they want to do is listen to a stumbling and bumbling teacher. So we talked to each other, picked at each other, squirmed and basically misbehaved much of the time in class.

Mr. Meek was just that ... he was meek. He would never get upset at us or confront us individually in class about our behavior. But he had a masterful plan that worked over time to bring law and order to the class time. You see, after each class he would draw one or two of us aside. His message was always simple and easy to understand ... "Do I need to talk to your parents about your behavior in Sunday School?" That put the fear of the Lord in each of us at least for a while. You see, when I was raised if the teacher, at church or school, threatened to talk to your parents it was serious business. You could expect some form of corporal punishment was on the way in addition to a formal personal apology to the teacher, usually with your parents present. Just thinking about what you faced would improve your behavior, at least for the rest of the day.

Yes, that is what Mr. Meek did. And guess what? It worked! He eventually got control of the class and never lost it the rest of the year.

Mr. Meek was still a terrible communicator, but he loved his class and wanted to see each of us saved. He showed up every week and never failed to tell us that Jesus loved us and wanted us to go to Heaven. However, the thing that I remember the most about him is that he was the person who confronted me about my need for eternal salvation. He told me that I could be saved through asking God to forgive me of my sins and praying to receive Jesus as my personal Lord and Savior. At Mr. Meek's continual prodding, I stepped out in our late spring revival on a Sunday morning during Sunday School seeking to be saved. It was a special service designed for children ready to turn their life over to Christ. I remember that special time as the evangelist, Dr. Don Berry, personally and individually led me to confess that I was a sinner in need of forgiveness and right then and there I asked Jesus to come into my heart.

That was fifty-seven years ago! Things have never been the same since. In the simple mind of a child I knew that I had accepted Christ and that I was "saved." That was good enough for me for a long, long time. I wasn't thinking about heaven and the **eternal life** that God had granted me when I was saved. But now on the other end of my lifeline here on earth, let me tell you that I get excited every time I think about what God has granted me … **eternal life** with Him in Heaven. Eternal life is longer than forever. It is infinite. It has no end. God is the Master of time! (If you haven't already done so, please see my recent article "In His Time" at this link: In His Time

God has written down my name on the Lamb's Book of Life and nothing can remove it … even physical death on this earth! Our church keeps a ledger of those members who have passed on to eternity. Fittingly enough, we call it **"The Glory Roll."** We have made a practice as we remove their name from our church roll of adding them to our Glory Roll. Of course, we clearly recognize that God had already written down their name in *His Glory Roll* when they were saved.

Scripture: (all NIV unless otherwise noted)

Luke 10:17-20 – *17 The seventy-two returned with joy and said, "Lord, even the demons submit to us in your name." 18 He replied, "I saw Satan fall like lightning from heaven. 19 I have given you authority to trample on snakes and scorpions and to overcome all the power of the enemy; nothing will harm you. 20 However, do not rejoice that the spirits submit to you, but rejoice that your names are written in heaven."*

Revelation 3:5 – *He who overcomes will, like them, be dressed in white. I will never blot out his name from the book of life, but will acknowledge his name before my Father and his angels.*

Revelation: 20:15 – *If anyone's name was not found written in the book of life, he was thrown into the lake of fire.*

Discussion:

In Luke 10 Jesus appoints seventy-two followers to send out two by two ahead of Him to every town and place where He was about to go (vs. 1). Jesus told them that the harvest of souls to be saved was plentiful but the workers were few. Their instructions were to make way for the coming of the Christ, to heal the sick, and move on to the next town if they were rejected. To their astonishment the seventy-tw0 returned to Jesus with great joy in their heart. They were ecstatic that even the demons had submitted to them. Jesus told them that that He had given them authority over the demons and that it was because of Him that they had no power over them. But the important thing that Jesus pointed out to these Christ followers is not related to the power over demons at all. Instead Jesus, with a joyful heart, says that they should be rejoicing because their name is written down in Heaven.

When you are saved, God writes your name down in "The Lamb's Book of Life." The "Lamb" is Jesus. It is His book. It is **God's Glory Roll**. The names of all those who are going to Heaven through the saving grace of Jesus Christ are written there and will be there for eternity. In Revelation 3:5 Jesus promised that He *"will never blot out"* the names of those who are saved and that He will acknowledge each of their names *"before My Father and his angels."* Their reward will be an eternity in Heaven.

The consequences for those whose name is not written in "The Lamb's Book of Life," **God's Glory Roll**, are also eternal. Revelation 20:15 tells us that they will spend their eternity in *"the lake of fire."*

Reflection:

I am so glad that as a twelve year old boy I accepted Jesus as my Savior. My name is already written down in Jesus' book. How about your name? Is it already written down in **"God's Glory Roll?"** If not and you want make sure that you to will spend your eternity in heaven, then just like Mr. Meek I am confronting you with this question: Is it time that you gave your heart and life to Jesus? Refer to the back of this book or follow this link for an outline of how you may do just that. How To Become A Christian.

I have a missionary friend in Europe who is home in the states as his mother is in her final days. He shared his prayer today with his supporters. I am certain that he would not mind me sharing it with you as well.

Dear Heavenly Father,

Thank you so much for <his Mom, name omitted> and for the many, many ways you have blessed me through her life. Now as she continues to hang on to this life by what seems like a thread, I ask that you glorify yourself in her final moments on earth and through her death, whenever you choose to call her HOME. I thank you for what awaits her...as Peter calls it...an inheritance that can never perish, spoil, or fade kept in Heaven for her...not to mention the godly loved ones and saints that have gone before her...the cloud of witnesses that might be watching and waiting for another daughter of God to finish her race and cross that finish line. May her welcome be becoming of the godly woman that she was and is.

And, Father, in your mercy reduce her suffering, and give grace to those of us caring for her and waiting for her to cross that finish line.

With a heart that is heavy and light at the same time I pray in the Name of the One who has already finished the race...my Savior Jesus Christ, Amen.

The mother of my missionary friend already has her name on **The Glory Roll**! It is this knowledge that gives my friend peace.

I sang in a southern gospel quartet for twenty years when I was younger. The name of the group was The Good News. We finally retired because most of us had too much on our plate to keep it going. As I wrote this article I couldn't help but think about one of the songs we recorded, "When I Get Carried Away." The song was exciting and we received a strong response every time we sang it. The audio of the song is available on YouTube at the following link:

When I Get Carried Away – The Good News

If you are online reading this article you can click on the above link to hear the song. I have included the lyrics below so you can see how it relates to this topic. Why not sing along or hum as you listen! The roll that the song refers to is **God's Glory Roll**!! I'm sure you can see why this song still excites me today. My name too is written down on **"God's Glory Roll."** Hallelujah and Amen!!

When I Get Carried Away

I'm gonna let the *glory roll* when the
roll is called in glory
I'll gonna get beside of myself when I get beside
the king that day
I'm gonna have the time of my life
when the time of my life is over
I'm gonna get carried away when I get carried away

Well, I don't know why I become a little shy
When I get around a whole lotta people
And I can't figure out why I never can shout
About the love that floods my soul
I must confess, I can't express
The feelings deep inside me

The things I know and cannot show
One day will overflow

I'm gonna let the *glory roll* when the
roll is called in glory
I'll gonna get beside of myself when I get beside
the king that day
I'm gonna have the time of my life
when the time of my life is over
I'm gonna get carried away when I get carried away

Well, I'll pass the clouds and shout so loud,
It may sound like thunder
My tearful eyes may fill the skies
Until it looks like rain
When I leave this world past the gates of pearl
And stand before my Savior
I let my soul let the **glory roll**
When from the roll He calls my name

I'm gonna let the *glory roll* when the
roll is called in glory
I'll gonna get beside of myself when I get beside
the king that day
I'm gonna have the time of my life
when the time of my life is over
I'm gonna get carried away when I get carried away

13 – A Recollection – Pine Lake Baptist Church Fire – June, 1996

Background:

Things aren't always as they seem on the *"first blush."* So there's no misunderstanding , here's how I am choosing to define *"first blush"* – at the first glimpse or impression; as in, "at *first blush* the idea possesses considerable intuitive appeal but on closer examination it fails." That is an important distinction for the reading of this article.

In 1996 the national news media was riveted on stories regarding church burnings primarily in the southern USA, and in particular the burning of black churches. One news outlet after another fell into the trap of *"first blush"* journalism. Articles flooded the airways and printed media regarding the burnings and characterized them as hate crimes against minorities, even terrorism fostered by white racists. ABC, CBS, NBC, and particularly USA Today and CNN ran continuous negative stories almost daily for a period of 5-6 months. Usually the stories received first place in the news broadcast or front page positioning in the printed media. This went on for months and was broadcast around the world.

The church burnings were eventually viewed as a national problem that had to be dealt with. According to the Chicago Tribune, even President Clinton took to the airways and said "This has got to stop, this tears at the very heart of what it means to be an American. ... We need every person from every walk of life and all faiths in America to speak up against this." Clinton even went so far as to meet with southern governors to "discuss strategies for stopping the attacks." Click on this link to a June 17, 1996 article to read more about the fire.

While there were indeed a lot of black church fires over that time-frame, there were many more white church fires as well. No journalist ever did enough homework over the 5-6 month period to check on what were thought of as "white" churches. Finally, when a fire destroyed the original sanctuary and education space building of the Pine Lake Baptist Church (PLBC) in Stone Mountain, Georgia things started to change and the "*first blush*" mania began to die down. PLBC was my church. Our congregation was now right in the bull's-eye of the international news media mania.

But PLBC was different as it was classified by the news media as a "white" church though the membership had long been multi-ethnic/multi-racial. Most reports in the national media now spoke of PLBC and the fact that "Pine Lake Baptist's congregation is mostly white, with about a dozen blacks out of 1,000 members." Of course, even this *first blush* comment was a gross exaggeration that the journalists just passed on to one another without really checking the facts. PLBC might have had 1,000 members on its roll, but just like so many other churches at the time of the article, only approximately 150-200 regularly attended the church. The other 800-850 had gradually moved away to other areas and never removed their names from the church rolls.

Since PLBC was still predominately white, the news media couldn't quite fit that into the perceived "*first blush*" pattern of southern black church burnings. So news media from all over the USA and some from even other parts of the world including the UK (BBC), Australia, Canada and some European countries descended on PLBC and the Pine Lake community to get the "scoop." The New York Times hired a writer/investigator that had covered a "hate" bombing of a Jewish Synagogue in Atlanta in previous years. She stayed on site at the church for more than a week interviewing dozens of members, and attending most of the church's meetings. She also did interviews with non-members from the surrounding community to check on PLBC's reputation. Her conclusion, the "supposed" terrorist burning of Pine Lake Baptist Church had nothing to do with racism, nor for that matter, terrorism.

Wow! Someone finally did enough digging to conclude something other than the perceived *first blush* conclusion. From that point forward the front page news story began to gradually fade away. PLBC, like so many other churches moved on to deal with the real tragedy — the loss of an important building to our ministry. The building was not used for administration as wrongly reported in the news media. It was actually now used as our children's facility where most of our sessions were conducted for boys and girls between the ages of six and twelve including our very successful weekly AWANA program. I will discuss more about this later in the article.

In December 1996 an <u>article by Michael Fumento</u> appearing in *The American Spectator* kind of summed up the media frenzy as Fumento looked back over the entire series of events and reported: *"in late June and early July — with the nation in the grip of a media blitz that was pushing public sentiment to the boiling point — USA Today pulled off the kind of once-in-a-lifetime journalistic coup that forges reputations and launches careers. Racism hadn't been a major factor in the burnings after all, the paper reported. Many more white churches were being torched, and the number of black churches set ablaze wasn't significantly higher than it had been in the past."* The article did a good job explaining that the feeding frenzy took place primarily because such stories sold papers and snared watchers ... the connection to deep-seated racial tensions, and supposed racial discrimination fueled the fire. Disinformation, made up statistics, conjecture, blowing the situation well beyond reasonable bounds, and down-right lies allowed the story to build and build to the point where facts didn't matter. *"First blush"* impressions and misleading information had won out over truth and honesty.

So why am I recounting this story in such detail? What is the point? Is there a Biblical application? The Bible has much to say about honesty (and dishonesty), integrity, half-truths, deception, innuendo, lies, slander, gossip, spreading rumors, and rationalization.

Scripture: all scripture ESV unless otherwise noted

Exodus 20:16 – *You shall not bear false witness against your neighbor.*

Galatians 6:7 – *Do not be deceived: God is not mocked, for whatever one sows, that will he also reap.*

1 John 1:8 – *If we say we have no sin, we deceive ourselves, and the truth is not in us.*

James 1:26 – *If anyone thinks he is religious and does not bridle his tongue but deceives his heart, this person's religion is worthless.*

1 Thessalonians 2:1-5 – *For you yourselves know, brothers, that our coming to you was not in vain. ² But though we had already suffered and been shamefully treated at Philippi, as you know, we had boldness in our God to declare to you the gospel of God in the midst of much conflict. ³ **For our appeal does not spring from error or impurity or any attempt to deceive, ⁴ but just as we have been approved by God to be entrusted with the gospel, so we speak, not to please man, but to please God who tests our hearts. ⁵ For we never came with***

words of flattery, as you know, nor with a pretext for greed—
God is witness.

Discussion:

My reference to Exodus 20:16 is clearly related to the topic. This is the ninth of God's Ten Commandments. Bearing false witness is more than lying in a courtroom. False witness is more than lying in general. False witness degrades one's reputation and dignity. Proverbs 6:16-19 (NIV) says - *"16 There are six things the Lord hates, seven that are detestable to him: 17 haughty eyes, a lying tongue, hands that shed innocent blood, 18 a heart that devises wicked schemes, feet that are quick to rush into evil, 19 **a false witness who pours out lies and a person who stirs up conflict in the community.** "*

In the case of the church fires in 1996 the news media was definitely a victim of the *"first blush"* syndrome. Sometimes we let our prejudices get in the way of the truth. What seemed to be true was not true at all. It was ultimately determined that only four of the eighty church burnings studied of black churches were racially motivated. Over the same period there were also 140 white churches burned and few of these were racially motivated. These statistics were purposefully ignored by the media, particularly USA Today, because they did not support their preconceived and daily hammered front page story line. However, the erroneous stories did stir up conflict in the community and all across the world. There are consequences to such misrepresentation and everyone suffers as a result. But don't be deceived ... Galatians 6:7 tells us that the sower of false witness information will ultimately be the reaper. The sower may argue that it was just a mistake, not a sin. But the Bible is clear about sin saying that we can easily fool ourselves (1 John 1:8). For the Christian James (James 1:26) teaches that we should bridle our tongue and not pass along misinformation and lies as it is in opposition to our religion and thus our witness.

To carry the analysis a little further, Christians in particular have a responsibility to speak the truth and not pass along false rumors, *first blush* impressions, unfounded accusations and flat-out lies. Far too often during the black church burning era national "religious" leaders fanned the flames of civil discontent by supporting and repeating the false stories. 1 Thessalonians 2:1-5 speaks to the Christian's responsibility to not let their motives and actions ... *"spring from error or impurity or any attempt to deceive [4] but just as we have been approved by God to be entrusted with the gospel, so we speak, not to please man, but to please God who tests our hearts."* This is good advice for everyone and going against this Biblical advice is exactly the way that false rumors and gossip are spread. You may want to refer to my article On Christians Spreading Rumors and Gossip in the Church.

Reflection:

At the time of the PLBC church fire in 1996, the retired Reverend Randy Mullis was our Interim Pastor while we searched for our new permanent pastor. Brother Randy held us together and kept us focused on the right things in a very difficult time. God knew both who and what we needed and He provided.

Brother Randy was the former pastor of Rainbow Park Baptist and Tucker First Baptist. He and his lovely wife Kathleen had the sweetest attitude. Randy's style of preaching depended heavily on his long life experience and he often told us personal stories related to his scripture lessons. In his late 70's, Randy would probably have just rather enjoyed his retirement than to take on another church. But God told him differently and sent him to us with a very specific purpose in mind. Randy was good-hearted, kind, always positive, flexible, and very experienced with multi-ethnic and multi-cultural congregations. Mrs. Kathleen was such a compliment to Randy with her radiant smile and sweet spirit. She fit right in with our people and quickly made friends with everyone.

Brother Randy spoke to the national and international media repeatedly about our church and the fire. No matter who called, he responded. He was professional and kind. He spoke calmly on camera with CNN and never once broke from his Christian character. I thank God to this day for Randy and Kathleen ... both now in Heaven with the Lord.

The real loss to our church as a result of the fire was the lack of adequate space to continue to conduct our active community serving Children's program. We never focused on self-pity. We were concerned about ministry. As it turned out, the building that burned was covered completely by insurance.

Pine Lake Baptist Church Children's Building

Over the next six months, contractors built a brand new Children's building with wonderful educational space, a half-court basketball space, and an area specifically suited to our AWANA program where children learned scripture and participated in activities that would guide them through rest of their lives. Some of the AWANA children ministered to in the succeeding years went on to become leading citizens in the community finishing college and even graduate school. Many of these children came from single parent homes. Some of their parents joined our congregation and are still a vibrant part of our church in 2012.

2008 Trunk or Treat for AWANA Children

How many children has the "tragedy" aided through the ministry of Pine Lake Baptist Church in the years after the fire? God blessed in the midst of a seeming tragedy … in the midst of false *first blush* impressions … in the midst of lies and false accusations … in the midst of a real need.

Adult Sunday School Christmas Party 12-20-2008

PLBC is still a multi-cultural, multi-ethnic church; however, we don't concentrate on that at all. We are simply a church focused on serving the Lord Jesus Christ and equipping the saints. Our people love each other and our church serves the community. I am proud to be a part of such a vibrant congregation. And I am glad that God used our church to help change the tide of the negative international media reporting in 1996 regarding the church fires. We have so much for which we are thankful. God has blessed our ministry and seen us through a number of major transitions.

Looking back some sixteen years later, I am thankful that the truth finally came out about the church fires. I am concerned that today's national news media has fallen even further away from reporting the news truthfully and factually. It appears that they are now focusing less on truth and more on opinion and support for their own agendas. God will not be mocked. There is a price to pay for arrogance, disinformation and lying.

Christian, make sure that you are doing what is right in the sight of God. Tell the truth; support your local church by not participating in the spread of half-truths, lies, gossip and rumors. Do not be deceived by *first blush* impressions. Remember, God expects Christians to live by His standard as recorded in His Word and not our fleshly desires.

14 – The Lost Generation

Background:

I read my daily <u>Open Windows</u> devotional for April 16, 2012 and was struck by the brevity and power of the message. This particular devotional was contributed by <u>Marvin Minton</u>, Senior Pastor, Crawford Road Baptist Church, Phenix City, Alabama. The entire devotion is included here for convenience. It will take only a couple of minutes to read it. It will be worth it. I'll add my thoughts in the **Discussion** and **Reflection** sections below.

The Lost Generation

Devotional Passage: Judges 2:6-11

And also all that generation were gathered unto their fathers: and there arose another generation after them, which knew not the Lord, nor yet the works which he had done for Israel. Judges 2:10

My father's wedding band was too large for me, so I hid it away in a jewelry box. As time passed, I put on weight, and my own wedding band grew tight. My wife suggested I wear my dad's ring until I could get mine resized. It fit perfectly!

When I looked at that ring, it reminded me I was my father's son. I looked, talked, and acted like him. His values, molded by the Great Depression and World War II, became my values through his influence. I think he would be proud to have me wear his wedding band.

Joshua's generation passed away, and their influence for the Lord died out. The new generation received material benefits from their parents but missed the spiritual connection vital to their continued success. Everyone in the kingdom of God has a personal spiritual birth certificate, so every upcoming generation is a potentially lost generation. What can leave our children to remind them of their spiritual heritage? Father, help me share Your love with the next generation.

Scripture: (all scripture KJV unless otherwise noted)

Judges 2:6-11 (focus on verse 10) - 6 *And when Joshua had let the people go, the children of Israel went every man unto his inheritance to possess the land. ⁷ And the people served the Lord all the days of Joshua, and all the days of the elders that outlived Joshua, who had seen all the great works of the Lord, that he did for Israel. ⁸ And Joshua the son of Nun, the servant of the Lord, died, being an hundred and ten years old. ⁹ And they buried him in the border of his inheritance in Timnathheres, in the mount of Ephraim, on the north side of the hill Gaash.* **¹⁰ And also all that generation were gathered unto their fathers: and there arose another generation after them, which knew not the Lord, nor yet the works which he had done for Israel.** *¹¹ And the children of Israel did evil in the sight of the Lord, and served Baalim.*

Discussion:

Judges 2:11 says it all ... once Joshua and his generation died the chosen people of God that had been given the Promised Land by Jehovah God **"did evil in the sight of the Lord."** One generation is all that it took for the followers to turn away from God and adopt the religions invented by man. The perverted generation that followed Joshua completely **lost** their way … not just in their worship of God, but they **lost** their way by trusting in life-values that were diametrically opposed to those given by God and taught to them by Moses and Joshua. They searched for answers in the wrong places with the wrong people and the wrong goals in mind. They became "**The Lost Generation**." They had completely forgotten what their ancestors had experienced when they turned away from God. Their "**lost**ness" resulted from direct disobedience of God's commands. They intermarried with unGodly foreigners that were not driven out of their land in accordance with God's specific instruction to their ancestors. They accepted the religious practices of their mates and surrounding neighbors losing all touch with God Almighty.

There were some who were still seeking to serve God and "**do what was right in the sight of the Lord**," but the vast majority of "**The Lost Generation**" ignored God's commands. They lived empty and useless lives serving other gods such as the Baals. They worshiped idols made with their own hands, not the God of universe that spoke everything into existence (including them). They could have cared less about The Ten Commandments … especially the first two that speak directly about having "no other gods before me" and making and worshipping "graven images" of gods.

What a sad commentary on the times. But, thank God that there was still a small remnant that continued to seek and serve the one and only true Jehovah God.

Reflection:

If you have read this far then you can't miss my point ... how different are we? We live in a world that is **lost**. The vast majority of our American people are **lost**. Our leadership is **lost**. Even our President appears to be **lost** as he supports popular and self-serving political policies that are directly opposed to God's Ten Commandments. My prayer today to the Lord God Almighty went something like this:

*"Lord, it appears that we are headed in the same direction as that traveled by **The Lost Generation** in the days following the death of Moses and Joshua. I pray that the current generation will not become another **Lost Generation** because my generation fails to speak up for and teach 'what is right in the sight of the Lord.' Empower me to be an instrument of Your will and speak boldly about You in my final years here on earth. In the wonderful saving name of Jesus, Amen and Amen!!*

Perhaps you don't know how you can be saved and exempt yourself from The Lost Generation. This link will help you know "How to Become a Christian" by accepting the free gift of salvation offered by Jesus Himself.

15 – God's Solution for Anxiety

Background:

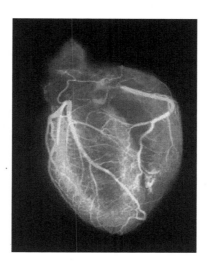

Angiogram of a Healthy Heart.
Photograph by SPL/Photo Researchers, Inc.

I have a serious heart condition. It has plagued me for the past twenty-two months since October, 2010. Specifically, my problems originate with the heart's electrical system and not with the blood vessels (coronary heart disease). The pumping function of my heart is strong. The electrical system that regulates the pumping function is erratic.

Doctors have concluded via a heart biopsy that my electrical problems were caused by an as yet unidentified virus that attacked my heart causing inflammation which resulted in scarring as the inflammation healed. The scarring interferes with the consistent transmission of the electrical signal across my heart, particularly in the lower ventricular chambers. The official medical terms for my condition are heart block, atrial fibrillation, ventricular tachycardia, and ventricular fibrillation. Over the course of many months, my doctors tried several medication combinations before settling on the current mix. I also underwent a ventricular ablation which cauterized a number of the worst offending tissues within my heart. As a result of these abnormal medical conditions, I have an implanted defibrillator/pacemaker that helps control my heart rhythm and delivers a shock to restart the heart in the event of a significant issue. I also take a number of strong medications to help control the various conditions.

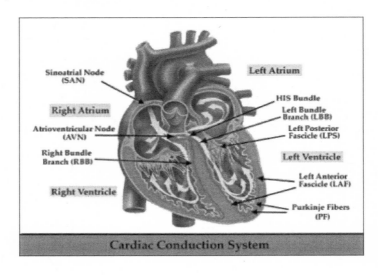

Marquette Electronics Copyright 1996

The good news is that things have recently settled down and I am making steady progress recovering with no significant heart incidents over the past three months. That was not the case for the previous six months. On the other hand, the medications have, at least in part, caused what doctors refer to as a "chemical imbalance" within my brain that affects the neurotransmitters (click the link for a detailed description of the function of neurotransmitters). This chemical imbalance contributes to a heightened level of *anxiety*. Admittedly, *fear* is also a contributor to my *anxiety* ... *fear* that my heart will stop, *fear* that I will receive another shock, *fear* that I might not be revived, *fear* that I might injure someone else if I pass out driving, *fear* that _____ (you fill in the blank).

It took a long while for me to admit that *fear* is really involved with my condition and interfering with my normalcy, but there is now no doubt in my mind about it. Early on I didn't believe that I was fearful enough to blame that for some of my issues. After all, I am a Christian under the perfect care of my Heavenly Father, the Almighty God, the Creator of all that was, is, and forever shall be ... the great "I Am." I trust in Him as my powerful protector and healer. What do I have to *fear*? Nothing is too hard for God. But after repeatedly discussing the situation with several of my physicians they convinced me that *anxiety* and fear are commonly involved in situations like mine. They recommended lowering my stress level, increased rest and some additional medications ... one of which I now regularly take and one which I don't take because of the additional side-effects that it caused. Sound familiar? My wife and I once worked through similar issues with one of my parents. It was a tough situation. I recall how fearful that parent was at times and how difficult it was to control the fears. Medicine helped sometimes, but not always.

Anxiety, Fear, Worry, Stress, Sickness ....

So, for the first time in my life I am dealing with long-lasting *anxiety* ... *anxiety* that in and of itself can cause serious physical, emotional and social problems. Fortunately, I serve an on-time, all-powerful God and am bound for an eternity in Heaven with Him because I have accepted His son Jesus as my Savior and Lord. God has provided direction for me in His Word, The Bible, on how to handle all of my life needs including *anxiety*. God is also using others to help me deal with this *anxiety* such as my wife, my son and my Christian friends. In addition, several months ago I was fortunate enough to view a sermon entitled Victory Over Anxiety presented by Dr. Charles Stanley, former President of the Southern Baptist Convention, Pastor of the First Baptist Church of Atlanta and founder of In Touch Ministries. That sermon and my diligent search of the scriptures have put me on a path to recovery using *God's Solution for Anxiety*. While this is still a work in progress, I wanted to share it with others as it is a sure method for His healing.

Scripture: (all Scripture NIV unless otherwise noted)

1 Peter 5:6-7 – *⁶Humble yourselves, therefore, under God's mighty hand, that He may lift you up in due time. ⁷Cast all your **anxiety** on Him because He cares for you.*

Philippians 4:4-7 - *⁴Rejoice in the Lord always. I will say it again: Rejoice! ⁵Let your gentleness be evident to all. The Lord is near. ⁶Do not be **anxious** about anything, but in every situation, by prayer and petition, with thanksgiving, **present** your requests to God. ⁷And the peace of God, which transcends all understanding, will guard your hearts and your minds in Christ Jesus.*

Matthew 6:33 – *But seek first his kingdom and his righteousness, and all these things will be given to you as well.*

Psalm 121:5-8 – *⁵The Lord watches over you — the Lord is your shade at your right hand; ⁶the sun will not harm you by day, nor the moon by night. ⁷The Lord will keep you from all harm — he will watch over your life; ⁸the Lord will watch over your coming and going both now and forevermore. The Lord will keep you from all harm — he will watch over your life; ⁸the Lord will watch over your coming and going both now and forevermore.*

Matthew 26:37-39 – *³⁷He took Peter and the two sons of Zebedee along with Him, and He began to be sorrowful and troubled. ³⁸Then He said to them, "My soul is overwhelmed with sorrow to the point of death. Stay here and keep watch with Me." ³⁹Going a little farther, He fell with His face to the ground and prayed, "My Father, if it is possible, may this cup be taken from me. Yet not as I will, but as You will."*

Hebrews 11:1, 6 – *¹ And now faith is confidence in what we hope for and assurance about what we do not see. ... ⁶ And without faith it is impossible to please God, because anyone who comes to him must believe that He exists and that He rewards those who earnestly seek Him.*

Matthew 6:25-34 – *²⁵ "Therefore I tell you, do not worry about your life, what you will eat or drink; or about your body, what you will wear. Is not life more than food, and the body more than clothes? ²⁶ Look at the birds of the air; they do not sow or reap or store away in barns, and yet your heavenly Father feeds them. Are you not much more valuable than they? ²⁷ Can any one of you by worrying add a single hour to your life? ²⁸ "And why do you worry about clothes? See how the flowers of the field grow. They do not labor or spin. ²⁹ Yet I tell you that not even Solomon in all his splendor was dressed like one of these. ³⁰ If that is how God clothes the grass of the field, which is here today and tomorrow is thrown into the fire, will he not much more clothe you—you of little faith? ³¹ So do not worry, saying, 'What shall we eat?' or 'What shall we drink?' or 'What shall we wear?' ³² For the pagans run after all these things, and your heavenly Father knows that you need them. ³³ But seek first his kingdom and His righteousness, and all these things will be given to you as well. ³⁴ Therefore do not worry about tomorrow, for tomorrow will worry about itself. Each day has enough trouble of its own."*

Psalms 139:16 – *Your eyes saw my unformed body; all the days ordained for me were written in your book before one of them came to be.*

Discussion:

Let's start by settling on a definition of *anxiety* as it relates to my situation and this article:

> "**Anxiety** is a painful or apprehensive uneasiness of mind usually over an impending or anticipated ill ... an abnormal and overwhelming sense of apprehension and fear often marked 1 by physiological signs (as sweating, tension, and increased pulse), 2 - by doubt concerning the reality and nature of the threat, and 3 - by self-doubt about one's capacity to cope with it." (Webster's New Collegiate Dictionary, Springfield: Merriam, 1981, p. 51).

This definition describes my situation perfectly with a slight modification. For the Christian, there is an element that is missing from this definition. I would modify the third point as follows:

> ... and, 3 - by self-doubt and lack of trust (faith) in God's power to cope with it.

In his sermon <u>Victory Over Anxiety,</u> Dr. Stanley said that overcoming *anxiety* is a "faith battle." I identify with that statement. In studying this statement I was led to Hebrews 11:1 and 11:6 where we are told that "*... faith is confidence in what we hope for and assurance about what we do not see. ... 6 And without faith it is impossible to please God, because anyone who comes to him must believe that He exists and that He rewards those who earnestly seek Him.*" Thus I conclude that God is not pleased with us when we hold on to our *anxiety* and worry.

Dr. Stanley also provided additional insight into the definition of *anxiety* from a Biblical perspective:

> "In the New Testament, the word **anxiety** means *to be distracted or pulled apart.* This is the opposite of peace, which means, *to be bound together.* It can also be defined as *dread, apprehension, and uncertainty* and can be caused by past events, present situations, or future possibilities. Sometimes, **anxiety** is a fear of not being in control. Situations over which we have no control make us feel vulnerable and cause us to worry."

Leaving God out of any healing process for the Christian is a huge mistake. God cares for you (1 Peter 5:6-7). Trying to cope with *anxiety* by self-will is a huge mistake. How then does the Christian avoid such mistakes? The Bible promises that God will provide His peace when we humble ourselves. As Dr. Stanley related, God gave us emotions, including *anxiety*, for good reasons. *Anxiety* allows us to recognize risks in advance and potentially avoid those risks. For example, if a grizzly bear was close by, we most certainly would be fearful. That's good. If we hold on to the fear long afterward, that may be bad, especially if that fear lingers and keeps us from our normal activities. When our firstborn comes into the world we have a flood of overwhelming joy. That's good. When we are ill and we worry about our illness without doing anything about it, that's bad. When we hold on to our *anxiety* unnecessarily, that's bad.

Philippians 4:6-7 provides a formula for dealing with *anxiety*: *"6 Do not be anxious about anything, but in every situation, by prayer and petition, with thanksgiving, present your requests to God. 7 And the peace of God, which transcends all understanding, will guard your hearts and your minds in Christ Jesus."* Being a mathematician by training, I like things to be well-defined. Formulas do that for me. So, the formula can be stated as follows:

God's Solution for Anxiety

If you have <u>trusted God's Son, Jesus Christ, as your Savior and Lord</u>, **then**

$X = a + b + c + d$, where **X** is *God's Solution for Anxiety*, *and*

- **a** = Do not be fret about or fear your **anxiety**
- **b** = Take your **anxiety** to God in prayer with a spirit of thanksgiving
- **c** = Turn over your **anxiety** to God and let Him handle it
- **d** = Receive the peace of God into your heart and mind to replace your **anxiety**.

We are to make our ***anxiety*** a matter of prayer recognizing that God has the power to deal with the root cause and relieve it on our behalf. We should make our prayers with an attitude of thanksgiving. The promise is that God will give us peace ... a peace that passes our human understanding. God will guard our innermost being (our hearts and minds) in the same way that he guards our souls. That is of great comfort to me personally!

Notice there is a prerequisite required for this formula to work for you (Matthew 6:33). First and foremost, you must a born again Christian. That's the only way it will work. There are several <u>links</u> in this article that will aid you in turning your life over to the Lord. For long-time Christians, why would we ever doubt that God would withdraw his upholding power from us after sustaining us through so many previous trials?

Christian, Almighty God accepts full responsibility for you and your welfare (Psalm 121:5-8). God knew you even before you were born. He already knows your outcome in this life and has written it in His book (Psalms 139:16).

Reflection:

Christ in the Garden of Gethsemane – Heinrich Hoffman

Even Jesus Himself suffered from *anxiety*. In Matthew 26:37-39 Jesus was facing His final hours before He was crucified on the cross. He took Peter, James and John aside from the other disciples and told them that He was "*sorrowful and troubled ... to the point of death.*" He left them there to "*... keep watch with Me*" and went" *... a little farther*" away from them into the garden. In agony He prayed "*My Father, if it is possible, may this cup be taken from me. Yet not as I will, but as You will.*" After that prayer, I believe that God's peace came over Jesus as never before and He was content to do whatever His

Father required, knowing fully that ALL of His *anxiety* had been assumed by Almighty God.

So *God's Solution for Anxiety* is not really that hard to apply to the Christian's life. It is a choice, a choice that we should make. Given that, here's a question I've asked myself: Why did it take me so long to turn over my *anxiety* to Him? I already knew these principles and that they worked. Why didn't I choose to apply them earlier in my recovery? Perhaps it was because "I" wasn't ready to turn my *anxiety* over to God. Clearly I had to get to the point where I quit trusting so much in doctors, medical procedures and devices and choose to put my trust fully in God to take my *anxiety* from me. I can report that I am still learning more about Him every day in my faith battle with my heart condition. I pray that I may reach the point that Jesus did when He prayed "... *Yet not as I will, but as You will.*"

If you are interested in additional study on this topic you can refer to this partial list of additional scriptures that I studied during my quest for God's Solution for Anxiety:

Philippians 4:13 – *I can do everything through him who gives me strength.*

2 Corinthians 12:9-10 – *9 But he said to me, "My grace is sufficient for you, for my power is made perfect in weakness." Therefore I will boast all the more gladly about my weaknesses, so that Christ's power may rest on me. 10 That is why, for Christ's sake, I delight in weaknesses, in insults, in hardships, in persecutions, in difficulties. For when I am weak, then I am strong.*

Matthew 7:7-8 – *7 "Ask and it will be given to you; seek and you will find; knock and the door will be opened to you. 8 For everyone who asks receives; the one who seeks finds; and to the one who knocks, the door will be opened."*

Hebrews 13:5 - *Keep your lives free from the love of money and be content with what you have, because God has said, "Never will I leave you; never will I forsake you."*

Proverbs 12:25 – *An* anxious *heart weighs a man down, but a kind word cheers him up.*

Psalm 34:4 – *I sought the LORD, and he heard me, and delivered me from all my fears.*

Proverbs 3:5-8 – *5 Trust in the Lord with all your heart and lean not on your own understanding; 6 in all your ways submit to him, and he will make your paths straight. 7 Do not be wise in your own eyes; fear the Lord and shun evil. 8 This will bring health to your body and nourishment to your bones.*

Philippians 4:19 – *And my God will meet all your needs according to his glorious riches in Christ Jesus.*

16 – On Class Warfare and Demonizing the Rich

Background:

Recently I wrote a brief post on one of the social media sites regarding an extremely well-publicized controversy that captured the national news media's attention for more than a week. I want to expand on that post and touch on a couple of related topics equally as controversial – *Class Warfare and Demonizing the Rich.*

Dan Cathy, President and COO of Chick-fil-A

The negative media blitz started after an <u>interview</u> with Dan Cathy, President and Chief Operating Officer of Chick-fil-A, appeared in ***Baptist Press*** on July 16, 2012. Same-sex marriage proponents seized the opportunity to promote their ungodly cause by viciously and cowardly attacking one of the finest Christian run companies in the entire world. The ungodly attacks sickened me and countless other Christians and non-Christians alike.

In the entire hubbub Chick-fil-A and the Cathy family stayed true to the Word of God and well above the temptation to respond in kind. The public showed overwhelming support for the company and family by patronizing in mass their local Chick-fil-A in a vote of appreciation on August 1, 2012. The company hasn't published sales figures yet but did report that sales hit an all-time one-day record.

Other than the obvious tactics under-girding the attacks by the same-sex marriage and gay community proponents, one in particular really troubles me - the deliberate attempt to classify the openly Christian Cathy family as a group of selfish rich bigots out of touch with reality, disinterested in supporting the communities they serve, and interested only in acquiring more wealth. This type of attack fits perfectly with the agenda of the Occupy Wall Street protestors and the class warfare tactics currently in use by one of the national political parties in their repeated "the rich don't pay their fair share" campaign rhetoric.

After some scripture references, I'll discuss this further below.

Scripture: (all ESV unless otherwise noted)

1 Timothy 6:17-19 – [17] *As for the rich in this present age, charge them not to be haughty, nor to set their hopes on the uncertainty of riches, but on God, who richly provides us with everything to enjoy.* [18] *They are to do good, to be rich in good works,* [19] *thus storing up treasure for themselves as a good*

foundation for the future, **so that they may take hold of that which is truly life.**

Matthew 6:19-21 – [19] *"Do not lay up for yourselves treasures on earth, where moth and rust[e] destroy and where thieves break in and steal,* [20] *but lay up for yourselves treasures in heaven, where neither moth nor rust destroys and where thieves do not break in and steal.* [21] *For where your treasure is, there your heart will be also."*

Matthew 6:24 – *"No one can serve two masters, for either he will hate the one and love the other, or he will be devoted to the one and despise the other. You cannot serve God and money."*

Matthew 19:23-24 – [23] *And Jesus said to his disciples, "Truly, I say to you, only with difficulty will a rich person enter the kingdom of heaven.* [24] *Again I tell you, it is easier for a camel to go through the eye of a needle than for a rich person to enter the kingdom of God."*

Discussion:

In 1 Timothy 6:17-19 Paul exhorts Timothy to provide a special message to those of great wealth. Timothy's message is quite appropriate for our topic. The rich are to recognize and avoid the temptations of sin that their wealth provides ... avoid succumbing to pride, acting haughty, thinking too much of themselves, acting puffed up. Their eternal confidence must not be placed in their wealth here on earth. Instead they are to lay up their treasures in heaven. This is a direct teaching of Jesus as recorded in Matthew 6:19-21. The focus on our earthly treasure is wrong and sinful when it becomes the object of our actions. Jesus did not teach that wealth in and of itself is sinful. Instead, He taught that the "love of money" and all that it entails is sinful (Matthew 6:24). The use of money can serve both God and Satan.

Depending on riches will not get the rich man nor anyone else into heaven (Matthew 19:23-24). Trusting Jesus as Savior and Lord is man's only hope for eternal life. Nothing we can do on our own will ever get us to heaven. Just like the common man, the rich are to see all of their possessions as God's gift to them … they are assigned as God's stewards of these possessions. "Everyone to whom much was (is) given, much will be required …" (Luke 12:48). Christians believe that EVERYTHING belongs to God. We are just His stewards. God expects all of us to be **good** stewards of His possessions. It is far superior for the Christian to be rich in good works.

Reflection:

It is easy to accuse and demonize the rich through class warfare. Class warfare has existed for thousands of years. Often times it was/is justified. Given time each of us could think of historical examples where class warfare was the source of great pain. Here are a few examples that came to my mind:

- The Russian Revolution in 1917 that led to the founding of the Soviet Union in 1922 – a single party socialist state that fell in 1991.
- Hitler's rise to power in Germany and the establishment of a one party Nazi dictatorship leading to World War II
- China's revolutions in 1911 and 1949 where tens of millions were killed when the masses were pitted against the ruling classes. A further note – I believe that China's current communistic/socialistic system is in danger of a near future class warfare battle – currently 98% of China's 1.3 billion people have less

than $7,600 equivalent USA annual income. Only 2% pay taxes because the government owns and controls most businesses.

- The French Revolution (1789-1789) – a "period of radical and social upheaval…"

Sadly, both the Democratic and Republican parties in the USA are currently engaged in class warfare rhetoric. The Democrats in particular seem to be basing much of their presidential election strategy on this tactic … attack the rich … repeat over and over that the rich are not paying their fair share … pit the masses against the "wealthy" minority, contend that small business did not "build" their own business … and on and on ….

I submit that the ugly and unGodly strategy of pitting the masses against the wealthy is based primarily on covetousness. In the Ten Commandments, the Bible clearly defines covetousness as a sin (see Exodus 20, especially verse 17). All tax systems are a form of wealth redistribution and most democratic governments use some form of taxation to accomplish it. Governments have to pay for their services and must have a way to raise revenues. But when the taxes become burdensome on a small percentage of the population you have to ask the question … is that "fair"? What is a "fair share" when it comes to taxation? Is it 0%, 10%, 15%, 28%, 33%, 39%, 50%, 70%, 90% or 100%? Perhaps I will write on that in a future article, but if you are interested in it now you can refer to this Wall Street Journal article. Suffice it to say that even taxing the top 10% of tax payers at a 100% tax rate, in other words taking everything they earn, won't cover the spending gap generated by the current administration. So it is an outright lie … and class warfare … to say that all of the USA fiscal problems can be solved by having the rich pay their fair share. Only God defines what is fair. God owns it all anyway and none of us will take any of our wealth with us when we leave this world.

So, how do I tie all of this up and link it back to my opening comments provided above in the "Background" section? Let's return to the attack of the Cathy family and their Chick-fil-A business. The interviewer for the Baptist Press article mentioned above pointed out to Dan Cathy that "some have opposed the company's support of the traditional family." Cathy responded with this exact discourse on traditional marriage:

> "Well, guilty as charged. We are very much supportive of the family — the biblical definition of the family unit. We are a family-owned business, a family-led business, and we are married to our first wives. We give God thanks for that. We operate as a family business ... our restaurants are typically led by families; some are single. We want to do anything we possibly can to strengthen families. We are very much committed to that. We intend to stay the course. We know that it might not be popular with everyone, but thank the Lord, we live in a country where we can share our values and operate on biblical principles."

That was the extent of Mr. Cathy's comments. Almost immediately Mr. Cathy's comments were twisted by those groups in support of same-sex marriage to grab media attention and further their "cause". In summing up the situation on July 27, 2012, CNN reported: "Proponents of same-sex marriage spread Cathy's comments, eventually creating a firestorm of criticism on social media, including assertions that his comments and position were bigoted and hateful." Political leaders in major cities like Chicago and Boston jumped on the criticism bandwagon saying they would block Chick-fil-A's expansion into their area, only later when confronted having to retreat from their unlawful positions. But, when fires start they can consume everything in their path. And in this case, that's what the same-sex proponents hoped would happen to Chick-fil-A. To the contrary, at the height of the controversy, Chick-fil-A experienced its busiest day ever on August 1, 2012 setting all-time sales records. This was in direct response to Mike Hukabee's (former Governor of Arkansas) call for a national Chick-fil-A Appreciation Day in support of the company and its Christian values. The response of the same-sex marriage supporters was to stage their "kiss in" at Chick-fil-A locations across the nation two days later. Though the media boasted about the response, it was basically a failure and soon after the controversy died down.

But one thing really struck me during the whole incident. It was the level of class envy and class warfare that the controversy aroused ... particularly against the Cathy family and their business success. Those who unmercifully attacked Dan Cathy for days on end know little about this fine man, his strong Christian values, his family nor their successful business. Some have even said and/or insinuated that Cathy is a hate monger who excludes those who do not agree with his religious position. Nothing could be further from the truth.

S. Truett Cathy – Founder, Chairman & CEO of Chick-fil-A

Original Dwarf House – founded 1946

The Cathy restaurant empire began with one small restaurant in 1946. After serving in World War II Dan's father, Truett S. Cathy, at the age of 25, and his older brother Ben, started the single location diner called the Dwarf Grill (later renamed the Dwarf House and still in operation at the same location today) located in Hapeville, Georgia. The restaurant operated 24 hours a day demanding a huge commitment from Truett and Ben. Ben tragically died two years later in a plane crash.

Truett continued successfully building the small business into a prosperous enterprise.

First Chick-fil-A location – Greenbriar Mall, Atlanta, Georgia

In 1967, twenty-one years after founding the Dwarf Grill, Truett opened his first Chick-fil-A restaurant in the Greenbriar Mall in south Atlanta. That location is still in operation 45 years later along with 1,615 other locations in 39 states and Washington D.C. with over 60,000 employees. What a small business success story ... made possible by the freedom we enjoy in the USA that is under threat by some in our current administration.

Early on Truett adopted a policy of closing on Sunday so he and his employees could worship at their local church. That policy still exists today. Few companies can boast that. The company is operated on Christian principles and those same principles permeate the private lives of the Cathy family.

In my opinion, the real hate mongers in this situation are those in opposition to the Cathy family and the Christian methods they employ in running their business. Some have even attacked Dan Cathy as a "rich billionaire white man" who **inherited** his fortune rather than working for it. By doing so, they have attempted to invoke class warfare among the races. They also complain that Dan and Chick-fil-A have exhibited a selfish lack of support for social causes. **What foolishness!**

Dan and brother Donald (Bubba) served as Dwarfs in their father's business.

Dan Cathy started his career in the family business at the age of nine singing songs to customers in his father's single restaurant. After graduating from college, Dan joined Chick-fil-A full-time in 1970. He personally led the opening of 50 Chick-fil-A locations across the US. He gradually worked his way up the ladder serving in significant positions in the business for thirty-one years before becoming President and COO in 2001. That doesn't sound like someone who **inherited** his wealth does it? I say it is full-blown covetousness in action.

I defy those nay-sayers to equal Dan Cathy's record of giving back to the community. As dedicated to Chick-fil-A business activities as he is, Dan also gives generously of his time, efforts and resources to the community. This is in accordance with the direct teachings of the Bible. Here's a partial list of awards, affiliations and associations derived from the Chick-fil-A website for Dan Cathy:

- Member, Board of Trustees, Berry College
- Member, Board of Trustees, Morehouse College
- Member, Advisory Board, Eagle Ranch
- Member, Advisory Board, Global Teen Challenge
- Executive Member, National Advisory Board, Lead Like Jesus
- Member, Board of Councilors, The Carter Center
- Member, Board Trustee, Gordon College Foundation
- Member, The New Hope Baptist Church (and trumpet player in the church band)
- Sunday School Teacher, 12th Grade Boys – Youth teacher for 37 years
- Member, Metro Atlanta Board of Directors, Chamber of Commerce
- Member, Jenkins Clinic Board of Directors, Vice Chairman
- Advisory Board, Heritage Preparatory School
- Recipient of the Outstanding American Award from the National Wrestling Hall of Fame – 2003
- Honorary Doctorate Degree from the State University of West Georgia, Anderson College and Carver Bible College
- Honorary Doctorate of Humanities Degree from Anderson College – 2005
- Honorary Doctorate from HBCA Entrepreneur Summit
- Honorary Doctorate, Law Degree, Pepperdine University, 2011
- And in his "spare" time, Dan earned his Airline Transport Pilot (ATP) license and has completed numerous marathons in Atlanta, Orlando, Los Angeles,

Boston and New York. Additionally, Dan is a passionate trumpet player, gardener and an avid motorcyclist.

The Cathy family also supports countless life changing ministries through its Winship Foundation.

Truett and Jeannette Cathy started WinShape Foundation in 1984. a non-profit organization and charitable foundation with a simple but profound goal: to help "shape winners."

The Cathy's original vision to encourage outstanding young people has greatly expanded over the last 20 years. The WinShape Foundation now supports a family of growing ministries, all driven by the same mission of shaping individuals to be winners.

The Cathy's ministries include the following:

- Winshape College Program
- Winshape Camps
- Winshape Homes
- Winshape Wilderness
- Winshape Retreat
- Winshape Marriage

- Winshape International

Chick-fil-A also provides scholarships to its employees. The Chick-fil-A Scholarship Fact Sheet lists some impressive stats: "Through its Leadership Scholarship program, Chick-fil-A has offered more than $29 million in financial assistance to more than 28,000 restaurant team members who have attended 3,168 colleges, universities and other educational institutions throughout the country. The company will award $1.65 million in scholarships to its restaurant team members in 2012."

A pretty impressive humanitarian record of serving the community I would say! Both the Cathy family and Chick-fil-A are living out God's commands. Thanks be to God for people and a company such as this. And phooey to those who attack these Godly people and their company to further their own selfish and covetous causes.

Further Reading and Study for those keenly interested in this topic:

- Read Dr. Albert Mohler's (President of Southern Seminary) 07-31-2012 blog on CNN's Religion blog site titled "Chick-fil-A Controversy Reveals Religious Liberty Under Threat"
- 1 Timothy 6:6-10
- 1 Kings 3:1-15 – Solomon's Prayer for Wisdom
- Proverbs 11:4
- Luke 12:13-21 – The Parable of the Rich Fool

Note to the casual internet user: All of the underlined words and phrases in this article are "links" to other internet pages. When you click on the "link" a new window will open and you will automatically be taken to that site. Close that window to return to this article.

17 – Pray With Confidence

Background:

When asked, most folks in the USA will say that they pray at least weekly (see "Who prays in a typical week?" statistics below). This is generally true whether or not they regularly attend a local church. People pray for a lot of reasons. Some pray because they don't know what else to do. Some pray out of duty. Some pray because they were taught to do so as a child. Some pray because of a specific need or desire. Some pray for our political leaders, our soldiers, the poor, and the helpless. Some pray because of sickness, financial problems, guilt, and uneasiness. Some pray for healing, wisdom, guidance, help with raising their children, strength to face a difficulty. Some pray on behalf of others. Some pray out of a spirit of thankfulness for God's blessings. Some pray to praise Almighty Jehovah God for who He is. Some pray for forgiveness. Some pray to receive Jesus Christ as their Lord and Savior and become a Christian. Sadly, some even pray for revenge and other improper reasons.

The Barna Group, founded in 1984, is a "leading research organization focused on the intersection of faith and culture." Barna has performed hundreds of surveys since their inception. A Barna survey completed prior to 2008 reports the following statistics:

Who prays in a typical week?

- 82% of adults
- 88% of women
- 75% of men
- 89% of teenagers
- 86% of those living in the South and Midwest
- 76% of those living in the West and Northeast
- 96% of born-again Christians
- 72% of people not describing themselves as born-again

Interesting statistics ... at least to me. Perhaps the most revealing statistic is the last one in the list ... nearly three-quarters of those who don't describe themselves as "born-again" still pray at least weekly. Why are they praying? Does God hear and answer the prayer of both the saved (born-again) and unsaved? If He does, what prayers does He hear and which ones does He choose not to hear. How can we be confident that God will hear and answer our prayers? How does one **Pray With Confidence**?

Scripture: (NKJV unless otherwise noted)

Jeremiah 32:16-19 – *16 "Now when I had delivered the purchase deed to Baruch the son of Neriah, I prayed to the Lord, saying: 17 'Ah, Lord God! Behold, You have made the heavens and the earth by Your great power and outstretched arm. There is nothing too hard for You. 18 You show loving-kindness to thousands, and repay the iniquity of the fathers into the bosom of their children after them—the Great, the Mighty God, whose name is the Lord of hosts. 19 You are great in counsel and mighty in work, for Your eyes are open to all the ways of the sons of men, to give everyone according to his ways and according to the fruit of his doings."*

Ephesians 2: 1-9 (NIV) – *1 As for you, you were dead in your transgressions and sins, 2 in which you used to live when you followed the ways of this world and of the ruler of the kingdom of the air, the spirit who is now at work in those who are disobedient. 3 All of us also lived among them at one time, gratifying the cravings of our flesh[a] and following its desires and thoughts. Like the rest, we were by nature deserving of wrath. 4 **BUT** because of his great love for us, God, who is rich in mercy, 5 made us alive with Christ even when we were dead in transgressions—it is by grace you have been saved. 6 And God raised us up with Christ and seated us with him in the heavenly realms in Christ Jesus, 7 in order that in the coming ages he might show the incomparable riches of his grace, expressed in his kindness to us in Christ Jesus. 8 For it is by grace you have been saved, through faith—and this is not from yourselves, it is the gift of God— 9 not by works, so that no one can boast. 10 For we are God's handiwork, created in Christ Jesus to do good works, which God prepared in advance for us to do.*

Matthew 7:7 – *"Ask, and it will be given to you; seek, and you will find; knock, and it will be opened to you.*

Discussion:

I started thinking about this topic after reading the April 27, 2012 devotional by Beverly Hill McKinney in Open Windows. It took a while to completely sink in and become personally relevant to me.

In Jeremiah chapter 32, Jeremiah was under "house arrest" by King Zedekiah of Judah because of his anger over Jeremiah's prophesy that Zedekiah and the people of Judah would soon fall in battle to Nebuchadnezzar, King of the Babylon, and would be carried away into captivity. Judah had repeatedly disobeyed God's laws and ignored God's pleas for repentance. Judah's cries for God's protection had come too late and His judgment on them was already in motion.

Bible History Online

Sample papyrus document for a grain loan. The land deed describing
Jeremiah's purchase of the field in Anathoth would have been prepared on
similar papyrus and placed in the sealed jar for safekeeping.

Through a vision from God and with His leadership Jeremiah purchased a field in Anathoth, (Jeremiah's home town) in the territory of the tribe of Benjamin. The original of the deed, properly executed and witnessed, was placed in a sealed jar that was given to Baruch, the son of Neriah, for safekeeping well into the future. The land purchase process signified "that though Jerusalem was (would be) besieged, and the whole country likely to be laid waste, yet the time would come, when houses, and fields, and vineyards, should be again possessed" (Matthew Henry's Commentary).

McKinney's Open Windows devotional relates that "... through this vision Jeremiah acknowledged God's greatness and showed nothing is too hard for Him. Certainly, the Creator, who spoke the heavens and earth into existence, has the power to do anything." This same God whom Jeremiah served is always there waiting on us to call on Him. **ALL** of our prayers offered to God are heard by Him. **None** are overlooked. This, in and of itself, is enough for me to pray more expectantly. Christians should **Pray With Confidence** recognizing that God has unlimited power to carry out His will in our lives when we let Him do so.

Ephesians 2:1-9 is a marvelously rich passage that is not usually associated with prayer. But I find one thought in particular extremely comforting in these verses. At the moment a seeker accepts Christ Jesus as personal Lord and Savior, Jesus enters and indwells the heart of the believer in the form of the Holy Spirit and **never leaves**. Previously and without the indwelling of the Holy Spirit we were sinners without Jesus, *"dead in your (our) transgressions and sins"* (vs. 1) ... following our fleshly thoughts and desires and *"deserving of wrath"* (vs. 3). *"**BUT** because of His great love for us"* (vs. 4) ... God *raised us up with Christ and seated us with Him in the heavenly realms in Christ Jesus (vs. 6)."*

WOW!! Christians have God indwelling in us and we are also simultaneously seated **in Christ Jesus** at the Father God's right hand. What a lofty position the Christian occupies in God's kingdom!! Knowing this Christian, why would you pray so timidly? By the Grace of God the Christian has been pulled up from the miry, fleshly clay and seated with Jesus. That is a powerful, powerful message!

In Matthew 7:7 Jesus told us to *"Ask, and it will be given to you; seek, and you will find; knock, and it will be opened to you.* So when offering your prayers to God, why would you do anything other than **Pray With Confidence**.

Reflection:

God indeed hears ALL of our prayers; both for the saved and unsaved (see Psalm 66:16-20). However, our "attitudes and actions can" easily sabotage our prayers. Sin, disobedience, hypocrisy, insincerity, wrong motives, lack of faith and even marital problems are among the saboteurs.

One of my dear brothers in Christ, Bernie Webb, is fighting Stage IV metastatic colon cancer. Bernie and I worked together for almost fifteen years through the 1980's and early 1990's. He was (and still is) a tremendous asset for the information technology team that supports a major international corporation. Bernie shares his daily journey in his blog, Believing IN Christ Jesus through ALL things. Bernie is a prayer warrior and I know that he prays with confidence. I point you to one article in particular, "God is able to accomplish INFINITELY more than we ask." Bernie shares his Christian faith and exposes his Godly courage and prayer life in this insightful article. I invite you to go to his site and read it.

In closing, one of my favorite praise choruses, *Ah Lord God,* speaks to the immeasurable power of God. Nothing, nothing, absolutely nothing, nothing is too difficult for God. Click on the link, watch the video and sing along with the words.

Ah Lord God

Ah Lord God, Thou hast made the heavens
And the earth by Thy great power;
Ah Lord God, Thou hast made the heavens
And the earth by Thine outstretched arm.

Refrain:
Nothing is too difficult for Thee,
Nothing is too difficult for Thee.
O, great and mighty God,
Great in power and mighty in deed,
Nothing, nothing, absolutely nothing,
Nothing is too difficult for Thee.

For those interested in additional reading on related topics please refer to:

- Is Anything Too Hard for God – jimdavenport.me
- God is Able to Accomplish Infinitely More Than We Ask – Bernie Webb, my friend and brother in Christ as posted in Believing IN Christ Jesus Through ALL Things. Bernie is battling active stage four colon cancer.
- Pray with Confidence – Beverly Hill McKinney: Published 04/27/2012 in Open Windows, a Lifeway Publication.
- Does God Ever Refuse to Hear Our Prayers – Bible Gateway Blog, 05-22-2012.

18 – If You Want to Hear God Laugh, Tell Him You Have a Plan

Background:

Recently my wife and I shared dinner with my former boss and ultimately my business partner, Steve, and his wife, Minnie. The fellowship was rich and we really enjoyed the time together as it had been more than a year since we had seen each other. We had talked on the phone and exchanged emails and messages many times. But that was not the same as being with each other in person. Steve is my very good friend, not just a business partner. Over the years our friendship has grown to a point of trust … a trust that embodies mutual respect and even compassion for each other. Steve and I enjoyed a long and successful business relationship. Our personalities are quite different, but I like to think that we fill in each other's gaps making each of us stronger. Steve has stood by me through some tough situations and I can never repay him, but only thank him deeply, for being such a good friend.

Steve is widely known for his strongly held opinions. Steve knows how to say "out loud" what others are thinking internally but will not say. He is also well-known for his self-descriptive sayings. I know that most of these sayings are not original with him, but he always seems to have the right quote at the right time to drive home a point. One of his favorite quotes that I first heard him utter twenty-five years ago is "If it looks like a duck, walks like a duck, and quacks like a duck … then it's a duck!" His point was as obvious then as it is today and I will never forget where I first heard it!

Over dinner as we were each discussing our grown children's lives and marveling at their rapid progress toward independence, Steve provided another of his appropriately timed sayings when he said "**If you want to hear God laugh, then tell Him you have a plan!**" This came at a time when we were discussing how our children and Grandchildren's lives and "plans" had quickly changed once they faced the reality that they, too, would soon become parents themselves.

I have thought about this saying repeatedly over the last month and have laughed along with God at myself and how many times I shared my plans with Him only to have Him in His great wisdom laugh at me and guide me to His plan instead.

Scripture: (all ESV unless otherwise noted)

Psalm 59:5-8 – *5 You, Lord God of hosts, are God of Israel. Rouse Yourself to punish all the nations; spare none of those who treacherously plot evil. Selah. 6 Each evening they come back, howling like dogs and prowling about the city. 7 There they are, bellowing with their mouths with swords in their lips— for "Who," they think, "will hear us?" 8 **But you, O Lord, laugh at them**; you hold all the nations in derision.*

Proverbs 1 :20-27 – The Call of Wisdom *20 Wisdom cries aloud in the street, in the markets she raises her voice; 21 at the head of the noisy streets she cries out; at the entrance of the city gates she speaks: 22 "How long, O simple ones, will you love being simple? How long will scoffers delight in their scoffing and fools hate knowledge? 23 If you turn at my reproof, behold, I will pour out my spirit to you; I will make my words known to you. 24 Because I have called and you refused to listen, have stretched out my hand and no one has heeded, 25 **because you have ignored all my counsel and would have none of my reproof, 26 I also will laugh at your calamity;** I will mock when terror strikes you, 27 when terror strikes you like a storm and your calamity comes like a whirlwind, when distress and anguish come upon you.*

Proverbs 2:1-5 – *1 My son, if you receive my words and treasure up my commandments with you, 2 making your ear attentive to wisdom and inclining your heart to understanding; 3 yes,* ***if you call out for insight*** *and raise your voice for understanding, 4 if you seek it like silver and search for it as for hidden treasures, 5* ***then you will understand the fear of the Lord and find the knowledge of God.***

Psalm 37:12-13 – *12 The wicked plots against the righteous and gnashes his teeth at him, 13* ***but the Lord laughs at the wicked,*** *for he sees that his day is coming.*

Psalm 2:1-6 – *Why do the nations rage and the peoples plot in vain? 2 The kings of the earth set themselves, and the rulers take counsel together, against the Lord and against his Anointed, saying, 3 "Let us burst their bonds apart and cast away their cords from us." 4* ***He who sits in the heavens laughs;*** *the Lord holds them in derision. 5 Then he will speak to them in his wrath, and terrify them in his fury, saying, 6 "As for me, I have set my King on Zion, my holy hill."*

Discussion:

While the saying "If you want to hear God laugh, tell Him you have a plan" didn't remind me of a specific scripture verse, it certainly seemed to me to be consistent with the Bible's teachings. Upon doing some research I found that the saying likely originated with an old Yiddish proverb more than a thousand years ago and perhaps even longer. Wikipedia has this to say:

"Yiddish (שיִידיש *yidish* or אשיידיש *idish*, literally "Jewish") is a High German language of Ashkenazi Jewish origin, spoken in many parts of the world. It developed as a fusion of Hebrew and Aramaic into German dialects with the infusion of Slavic

153

and traces of <u>Romance languages</u>. It is <u>written</u> in the <u>Hebrew alphabet</u>."

The Yiddish proverb is "Men tracht und Gott lacht." Roughly, this is translated as "Men plan and God laughs." In relatively recent times the proverb has made its way into some popular songs. Comedy writer and movie director Woody Allen is also credited by some with originating the saying, but it is clear to me that Allen drew from his Jewish heritage and teaching to somewhat popularize this saying.

The Bible does have a number of relevant scriptures on the subject. In Psalm 59:5-8 the writer implores God to "... *Rouse Yourself to punish all the nations; spare none of those who treacherously plot evil.*" The Psalmist then continues that as a result of their plotting (and planning) "***But you, O Lord, laugh at them;*** *you hold all the nations in derision.*"

Solomon speaks of the laughing of God in The Call to Wisdom recorded in Proverbs 1:24-26a quoting Him as saying – "*[24] Because I have called and you refused to listen, have stretched out my hand and no one has heeded, [25] because you have ignored all my counsel and would have none of my reproof, [26] I also **will laugh at your calamity** ...*" When we make our plans independent of God, the scripture tells us that God laughs at us knowing that apart from Him our plans will fail. Additional verses like Psalm 2:1-6 and Psalm 37:13 records the consequences to "nations" for planning and attempting to execute their plans without God saying: "***He who sits in the heavens laughs;*** *the Lord holds them in derision* (Psalm 2:4)." And further in Psalm 37:13 (NIV) – "*but the Lord laughs at the wicked, **for He knows** their day is coming.*"

Reflection:

As an example of how God thinks differently than man on many subjects, consider the following scripture passage dealing with the sin of partiality from James, the brother of Christ:

James 2:1-5: [1] My brothers, show no partiality as you hold the faith in our Lord Jesus Christ, the Lord of glory. [2] For if a man wearing a gold ring and fine clothing comes into your assembly, and a poor man in shabby clothing also comes in, [3] and if you pay attention to the one who wears the fine clothing and say, "You sit here in a good place," while you say to the poor man, "You stand over there," or, "Sit down at my feet," [4] **have you not then made distinctions among yourselves and become judges with evil thoughts?** [5] Listen, my beloved brothers, has not God chosen those who are poor in the world to be rich in faith and heirs of the kingdom, which he has promised to those who love him?

What we see at work in these verses is God dealing with the personal prejudices and sinful partiality of those Jewish Christians in the Jerusalem church. Jesus spoke to this in His Sermon on the Mount in Matthew 5:3 when He said *"Blessed are the poor in spirit, for theirs is the kingdom of heaven."* Isn't this just the opposite of what man would think? It seems that God is in the business of disrupting our lives … taking us off our planned courses … teaching us that His way, not our way, is His will for us. **If you want to hear God laugh, tell him you have a plan** … especially if your plan is not in keeping with His plans. Never be too timid or afraid to follow God's plans. Rest assured that His plans for you far exceed anything we can conjure in our limited human minds.

As a final note, consider The Plan of Salvation. If humans had developed this plan you can count on it that it would not be "free" and available to all. Instead, it would include a list of things that one has to accomplish before he is granted eternal life. Thankfully, that is not what God requires of us! I can just see Him laughing at the countless millions on this earth who are trying to work their way into His Heaven!

Heavenly Father, praise you as the creator and owner of everything that was, is, and shall be! Forgive me for trying to impose on you my plans. Help me to discover your plans for me and give me the courage to follow behind you and execute those plans. In the strong name of Jesus, Amen.

Related Links and Articles:

- In His Time
- Lifestyle Choices and Biblical Truth
- Seven Keys to Successful Christian Living
- "Do!" – A Call to Right Christian Action
- The Believer's Sufficiency in Christ
- In His Own Image
- How to Become a Christian

Related Southern Gospel Music by The Good News:

- <u>The Plan of Salvation</u>
- <u>Listen to The Good News</u>

19 – An Attitude of Thanklessness

Background:

Over the past six months I have written a number of articles on thankfulness and thanksgiving. Possessing An Attitude of Thankfulness is a rich blessing for the Christian. Thankfulness is a positive response to the grace of God. But there are times for all of us, even Christians, when it is really difficult to be thankful. Think about ... the times of rebellion by a wayward teenager ... the children that have to live through the their parents nasty divorce ... the father who has small children, has lost his wife to cancer, and is attempting to carry on a normal life ... the parents who are grieving over the loss of their son or daughter due to a tragic and senseless automobile accident caused by a drunk driver ... the wife who sees no way out of her physically abusive marriage. The list could go on endlessly. These are certainly examples of times in our lives where it would be difficult to be thankful. Such times can bring on a temporary state of great sorrow and distress. But God always understands our situation and is ready to provide us His unparalleled healing, comfort and loving kindness. Even in the toughest of situations Christians can and should be thankful for God's manifold blessings.

So, what is meant by the term "thanklessness?" Thanklessness is the opposite of thankfulness. Thanklessness is a negative response to God's grace. Thanklessness is the failure or refusal to acknowledge the receipt of something good. Continued thanklessness is ungratefulness, the wanton and deliberate lack of appreciation, ingratitude. Thanklessness is rude, offensive, discourteous, and crude. Thanklessness shows great disrespect, disregard. Thanklessness reveals the selfish and hateful side of our human nature. Thanklessness results in bitterness, grumbling, complaining.

Here are some scriptures to consider regarding our topic.

Scripture: (all ESV unless otherwise noted)

Jeremiah 1:16 – *[16] And I will declare My judgments against them, **for all their evil in forsaking Me**. They have made offerings to other gods and **worshiped the works of their own hands**.*

1 Chronicles 5:26 – ***So the God of Israel stirred up the spirit of Pul king of Assyria**, the spirit of Tiglath-pileser king of Assyria, and he **took them into exile**, namely, the Reubenites, the Gadites, and the half-tribe of Manasseh, and brought them to Halah, Habor, Hara, and the river Gozan, to this day.*

Romans 1:21 – *[21] For **although they knew God**, they **did not honor Him as God or give thanks to Him,** but they became **futile in their thinking**, and their **foolish hearts were darkened**. [22] **Claiming to be wise, they became fools**, [23] and exchanged the glory of the immortal God for images resembling mortal man and birds and animals and creeping things. [24] **Therefore God gave them up** in the lusts of their hearts to impurity, to the dishonoring of their bodies among themselves, [25] because they **exchanged the truth about God for a lie** and worshiped and served the creature rather than the Creator, who is blessed forever! Amen. [26] **For this reason God gave them up** to dishonorable passions. For their women exchanged natural relations for those that are contrary to nature; [27] and the **men likewise gave up natural relations with women** and were **consumed with passion for one another, men committing shameless acts with men** and receiving in themselves the due penalty for their error. [28] **And since they did not see fit to acknowledge God, God gave them up to a debased mind to do what ought not to be done**.*

Discussion:

Thanklessness is in short ... a serious sin. Thanklessness dishonors Almighty God, places the focus on man and can lead to serious consequences. Scripture records many historical instances where God's chosen children, the Hebrews, were at various times in their history continually thankless (תודה כפוי – Hebrew) and suffered greatly for their thanklessness.

In the seventh century BC the prophet Jeremiah, along with others, wrote of the impending doom that Judah faced at the hands of the Assyrians. Jeremiah said in chapter 1 verse 26 that God would declare *"judgments against them, **for all their evil in forsaking** ..." "They have made offerings to other gods and **worshiped the works of their own hands**."* The resulting Assyrian captivity of Israel in 722 BC is one prime example of how continual thanklessness for God's blessings, at least in part, caused the fall of the ten northern tribes (for example, see 1 Chronicles 5 and particularly 5:26). These ten tribes became known as the "lost tribes," the tribes that would remain in captivity for generations and not re-establish their promised homeland.

A Roman Coin minted in 56 AD Depicting Nero. This is thought to be the same year that Paul wrote his letter to the Romans.

Paul wrote his letter to the Roman Christians in approximately 56 AD during his third visit to the city of Corinth (See 2 Corinthians 13:1, Acts 20:2). Paul's letter anticipated his future visit to Rome where, according to The New Scofield Reference Bible published in 1967, he intended to communicate "the great doctrines of grace that had been revealed to him." In the very first chapter Paul explains the folly, foolishness and results of Gentile unbelief in Almighty God. In Romans 1:21 Paul points out their thanklessness, their vain imaginations and their darkened hearts. Paul goes on in verse 22-23 to say they claimed to be wise but were actually "fools" exchanging *"the glory of the immortal God for images"* of mortal man, birds and animals, the results of which were that ***"God gave them up*** *in the lusts of their hearts to impurity ..."*

I contend that this is exactly where the United States is today as a nation. We have legislated immorality, glorified homosexuality and even legalized same-sex marriage all the while persecuting Christians and totally ignoring the teachings of the Word of God. We have legalized and often federally funded abortion, willfully terminating the lives of God's helpless unborn human creations. There are severe consequences to our sin and in particular for our thanklessness both as individuals and as nations.

Reflection:

Dr. Billy Graham's November 1, 2012 article "America Under Judgement" appearing in Decision Magazine speaks directly to the results of our nation's thanklessness.

> *"Why is there such an increase of trouble for America? Could it be that our sins are beginning to catch up with us? Centuries ago Moses warned Israel that if she*

served God she would be the most blessed of all nations, but if she disobeyed God, terrifying judgment would come. In Deuteronomy 28:65-66, Moses warned: "And among those nations you shall find no rest, nor shall the sole of your foot have a resting place; but there the Lord will give you a trembling heart, failing eyes, and anguish of soul. Your life shall hang in doubt before you; you shall fear day and night, and have no assurance of life.

Moses warned that the enemies of Israel would conquer her if she disobeyed God. We all know the history of Israel. We know that Israel did disobey God and that she suffered one judgment after another.

Today America is following the same dangerous path. We worship the gods of secularism and materialism. God is displeased, and I warn you that His anger is being kindled. If ever a nation has enjoyed prosperity and the blessing of God, it is America; but instead of giving thanks to God, we have offered our reverence and worship to created things. As Paul wrote in Romans 1:20-21, "There is therefore no possible defense for their conduct; knowing God, they have refused to honor him as God, or to render him thanks. Hence all their thinking has ended in futility, and their misguided minds are plunged in darkness" (NEB).

Could this be the difficulty with some of our leaders today? Has all the planning of the past few years by some of America's most brilliant intellects begun to end in futility?

The Apostle Paul said, "They boast of their wisdom, but they have made fools of themselves." Then comes the awful judgment—"For this reason God has given them up to the vileness of their own desires" (Romans 1:21, 24, NEB). In other words, the Bible says there will come a day when a nation sins so much against God that God will give them up, and will allow them to go on for a time in pleasure, worldliness, idolatry, wickedness and immorality. The Scripture says that there is pleasure in sin for a season (Hebrews 11:25), but warns that the pleasure will be extremely short-lived and that judgment will follow."

Christian, when faced with great difficulty, valleys of loneliness, or seemingly insurmountable mountains to climb … don't despair. Don't get caught in a state of thanklessness. Realize that Jehovah God is in control. Believe in Him and His goodness. After all, He just may have chosen you for a very special assignment … an assignment that no one else could perform for Him. He knitted you together in the womb. He knows and controls every cell of your body and mind. God is good … *"Give thanks to the Lord, for he is good, for his steadfast love endures forever"* (Psalm 136:1).

An attitude of thanklessness takes our focus away from the Lord promoting pettiness and occupation with self, people, and problems which in turn cause depression and ultimately hopelessness. Let us place our focus on living as God's children instead of the world's children. A thankful child of the Father depends on Him and His triumph over sin. God is not the author of thanklessness. God is the author of thankfulness.

Father, forgive me when I allow my desperation to bring on a state of bitterness and thanklessness. Give me the strength to face the ups and downs of life with the sweet knowledge that God is good and will supply all of my needs. May I ever be found faithful and thankful for your promises. In Jesus Name, Amen and Amen.

Related Links and Articles:

- America Under Judgement

20 – God Will Provide

Background:

Troubled Times

Sometimes troubles are known well in advance. Sometimes troubles come completely as a surprise. Troubles are often the result of our bad decisions. Troubles can be minor. Troubles can be major. Troubles can pierce the very soul of man. However, troubles are sometimes the prelude to opportunity … opportunity to triumph over adversity … opportunity to gain a better understanding of ourselves and others … opportunity to face a problem head-on … opportunity to allow God to take over a situation for us … opportunity to help someone else through their similar troubles … opportunity to give glory to God for His great loving kindness.

Christian, I have good news upon which you can rely. Whatever the situation might be, God is in control. God always hears your prayers. God always has THE answer for ALL of your troubles. **GOD WILL PROVIDE!!**

At the conclusion of this article you will find a link to a song. I strongly encourage you to listen. It will encourage your heart! (You can **listen now** and come back here after it has finished if you prefer … but it would be best to wait. Don't miss the song.)

Scripture: (all scripture ESV unless otherwise noted)

Psalm 46:1 – *"God is our refuge and strength, a very present help in (times of) trouble. "*

1 Peter 5:6-7 – [6] Humble yourselves, therefore, under the mighty hand of God so that at the proper time he may exalt you, [7] casting all your anxieties on him, because he cares for you.

2 Corinthians 1:3-4 – *[3] Blessed be the God and Father of our Lord Jesus Christ, the Father of mercies and God of all comfort, [4] who comforts us in all our affliction, so that we may be able to comfort those who are in any affliction, with the comfort with which we ourselves are comforted by God.*

Psalm 34:17 – *When the righteous cry for help, the Lord hears and delivers them out of all their troubles.*

Psalm 56:8 (MSG) – *You've kept track of my every toss and turn through the sleepless nights, each tear entered in your ledger, each ache written in your book.*

John 16:33 – *I have said these things to you, that in me you may have peace. In the world you will have tribulation. But take heart; I have overcome the world.*

John 14:27 – *Peace I leave with you; my peace I give to you. Not as the world gives do I give to you. Let not your hearts be troubled, neither let them be afraid.*

Hebrews 2:17-18 – *[17] Therefore he had to be made like his brothers in every respect, so that he might become a merciful and faithful high priest in the service of God, to make propitiation for the sins of the people. [18] For because he himself has suffered when tempted, he is able to help those who are being tempted.*

2 Corinthians 12:7-9 – *⁷ So to keep me from becoming conceited because of the surpassing greatness of the revelations, a thorn was given me in the flesh, a messenger of Satan to harass me, to keep me from becoming conceited. ⁸ Three times I pleaded with the Lord about this, that it should leave me. ⁹ But he said to me, "My grace is sufficient for you, for my power is made perfect in weakness." Therefore I will boast all the more gladly of my weaknesses, so that the power of Christ may rest upon me.*

Proverbs 3:5-6 (NKJV) – *⁵ Trust in the Lord with all your heart, And lean not on your own understanding; ⁶ In all your ways acknowledge Him, And He shall direct[a] your paths.*

Philippians 4:6-7 – *⁶ do not be anxious about anything, but in everything by prayer and supplication with thanksgiving let your requests be made known to God. ⁷ And the peace of God, which surpasses all understanding, will guard your hearts and your minds in Christ Jesus.*

Discussion:

God Knows
God Cares
God Will Provide

God knows about each and every one of our troubling situations. As my Pastor, Dr. Keith Pisani, often says … God Knows, God Cares! God has already worked it out and is just waiting for us to get on board. The Bible teaches that *"God is our refuge and strength, a very present help in (times of) trouble" (Psalm 46:1).* We can be assured that God is our Deliverer, our Rescuer, our Redeemer! There is no need to hold on to our troubles. Instead, The Bible teaches us to turn ALL of our troubles over (ALL of your anxieties, ALL of your worries, ALL of your concerns) to our Heavenly Father. God cares for man (His unique creation in His own image) like no other (1 Peter 5:6-7). <u>In His Time</u> **God Will Provide** His matchless comfort (2 Corinthians 1:3-4).

King David was continually tormented by His troubles. David often wrestled with himself and with the Lord. But David had a heart for God and God loved David. Even in the midst of David's sleepless nights God was there. In Psalm 56:8 (MSG) David recorded *"You've kept track of my every toss and turn through the sleepless nights, Each tear entered in your ledger, each ache written in your book."* As a young husband and father I can remember many sleepless nights tossing and turning, worrying about financial challenges and all sorts of troubles. Looking back now I can see how God was working on me in every one of those situations. God was always there. God always provided. God was sufficient for my every need. Based upon a lifetime of experiences, it is with great certainty and God's peace that passes understanding (John 16:33, John 14:27) that I am able to say: **God Will Provide** for the Christian in every situation.

The Bible teaches that it was necessary for Jesus to be *"made like his brothers in every respect, so that He might become a merciful and faithful high priest in the service of God, to make propitiation* (the reconciliation) *for the sins of the people. For because He himself has suffered when tempted, He is able to help those who are being tempted"* (Hebrews 2:17-18). No one ever cared for you like Jesus! In the second form of the Holy Trinity, Jesus, and thus God, was tempted and suffered. Jesus overcame every temptation. God is able to help you overcome all circumstances. Jesus suffered and He overcame that suffering. God understands your suffering. God's care is sure. God's steadfast love is unfailing. God's promises are secure. **God Will Provide.**

Reflection:

The Bible records that the Apostle Paul suffered from a chronic physical affliction. We aren't told the nature of the affliction but we know that it was a chronic condition that often kept Paul from his work as a tent maker. Paul pleaded three times with God (2 Corinthians 12:7-8) to take the affliction away, but God chose not to heal Paul telling him instead *"My grace is sufficient for you, for my power is made perfect in weakness."* (2 Corinthians 12:9a). Oh my! His power, that is ... God's power, is made perfect in our weakness! Oh that I could say along with Paul: *"Therefore I will boast all the more gladly of my weaknesses, so that the power of Christ may rest upon me"* (2 Corinthians 12:9b).

Facing your troubles and stressful circumstances on our own is futile. I have heard both professional counselors and amateur psychologists say that the solution to dealing with all of our anxieties is to improve our coping skills. Instead of just learning to cope, why not just *"Trust in the Lord with all your heart, And lean not on your own understanding"* (Proverbs 3:5-6). God knows! God cares! **God Will Provide!**

A personal note is appropriate at this point. Twenty-seven months ago, three months after I retired from active full-time work of almost 50 years, I experienced a significant health issue. That issue drastically changed my everyday life. I had never been seriously ill. Then in one day all that changed. At first I wondered if I would be able to do those things that my wife and I had planned to do in retirement. My illness seemed to severely limit those plans. However, the health issues allowed me to learn that God had something else in mind for my future. With my physical activity limited, God turned me toward Christian writing. At first I planned only to write a few personal articles to pass along to my children, grandchildren and future family generations. But God changed my vision almost immediately. He led me to start a blog site. He then led me to publish a book, then another. I soon will publish my third book. God taught me through this experience that my health problem had a very specific purpose. God was laying an opportunity of a lifetime at my feet. I was convicted that He wanted me to take the trouble and turn it into a triumph. The writing has worked out to be a lifetime dream fulfilled. God knew. God cared. **God provided!**

Friend, will you trust God to provide for you? He had for me and He will for you. If you haven't yet accepted God as your

Savior will you do so now? I have a helpful section on my blog site on how to "Become A Christian." There is really nothing you can do on your own to secure God's promise of eternal life. God has already done that for you through Jesus Christ. Even in your need to be saved, God knows, God cares, **God Will Provide**.

Here is a wonderfully performed song by Gold City that will encourage your soul. By all means, listen to the gospel in song by clicking the following link: **God Will Provide**.

Additional Scriptures for Your Times of Trouble:

For Times of Trouble from http://www.familylife.com – Day 3 of God Has Not Forgotten You

- The death of a loved one – Matthew 5:4; Psalm 116:15; 2 Corinthians 5:8
- Facing a terrible illness – Psalm 103:3; Isaiah 53:5; Jeremiah 17:14; Matthew 26:39
- The separation of family members – Ephesians 3:20
- The loss of your job, home, and other possessions – Philippians 4:19; Matthew 6:31-34
- Financial troubles – Psalm 34:10; Joshua 1:8; Luke 6:38
- The fear of all you have yet to deal with – Isaiah 41:10
- The destruction of your beloved city or community – Isaiah 58:12

Related Links and Articles:

- When Trouble Knocks
- God Has Not Forgotten You

Appendix A – How to Become a Christian

Here are the steps that you need to follow to **become a Christian**:

- **Realize that you are "lost" – totally estranged from God and separated from God by a sinful nature.** *(Romans 3:23 – For all have sinned and come short of the glory of God.)*
- **Acknowledge that sin deserves punishment.** *(Romans 6:23 – For the wages of sin is death, but the gift of God is eternal life through Jesus Christ our Lord.)*
- **Acknowledge that Jesus took the punishment for your sins by dying on the cross.** *(Romans 5:8 – But God demonstrated his love toward us, in that while we were yet sinners, Christ died for us.)*
- **Ask Jesus to forgive you of your sins and come into your life.** *(Romans 10:9 – That if thou shalt confess with thy mouth the Lord Jesus, and shalt believe in your heart that God has raised him from the dead, you shall be saved.)*

The way we communicate with God is through prayer. You can use the following prayer as your own or pray one that contains these elements:

"Dear God, I admit that I am a sinner. I recognize that I deserve punishment. I also know that you died for my sins and that you were raised from the dead. I turn from self and sin and trust You to be my Savior and Lord. Take control of my life and help me to be the person that you want me to be. Save me now and save me forever. Thank You, Lord, for hearing my prayer and saving my soul. In Jesus' name, Amen."

God promises in the Bible that anyone who accepts Jesus as Lord will be saved. (Romans 10:13 – *For whosoever shall call upon the name of the Lord shall be saved.*) If you prayed the above suggested prayer and meant it, you can be assured that God has saved you. The Bible offers many other words of assurance about your salvation. One of the clearest descriptions of that assurance can be found in 1 John 5:11-13 – *And this is the record, that God hath given to us eternal life, and this life is in his Son. He that hath the Son hath life; and he that hath not the Son of God hath not life. These things have I written unto you that believe on the name of the Son of God; that ye may know that ye have eternal life, and that ye may believe on the name of the Son of God.*

If you need further explanation refer to this link: <u>More help on How to Become a Christian</u>. There you will find additional resources that will assist you in finding a local church. An email address and phone number is also supplied to assist you with your journey to become a follower of God and spend your eternity with Him in Heaven.

Appendix B – List of Links

The following table contains a list of the embedded links referenced in this book that are neither visible nor "clickable" in a hard copy format. The embedded links refer to specific URL's that make navigation in an online environment much easier and do not significantly interrupt the flow of the document. The links are listed in the order that they appear in the book. If you are internet savvy then you enter the link into your browser for additional information.

It should be noted that over time some of these links may move or be deleted. All were current as of the November, 2014 publishing date.

..... 01

Wikipedia►
http://en.wikipedia.org/wiki/Hallel

chesed►
http://en.wikipedia.org/wiki/Chesed

Boundless Love►
https://www.youtube.com/watch?v=TXPesWQmjAw&feature=youtube_gdata

Listen to The Good News►
http://jimdavenport.me/the-good-news/

..... 02

Hurricane Sandy►
http://en.wikipedia.org/wiki/Hurricane_Sandy

The storm turned deadly▶
http://www.cnn.com/2012/10/24/world/americas/tropical-weather-sandy/index.html

a hurricane/winter storm hybrid▶
http://www.huffingtonpost.com/2012/10/30/hurricane-sandy-storm_n_2042815.html

power outages▶
http://www.nydailynews.com/new-york/hurricane-sandy-death-toll-reaches-74-article-1.1195335

74 in the USA and still rising as of November 3, 2012▶
http://www.nydailynews.com/new-york/hurricane-sandy-death-toll-reaches-74-article-1.1195335

'A loss for everybody': Communities start cleanup after Sandy▶
http://www.cnn.com/2012/10/31/us/tropical-weather-sandy/index.html

Military and emergency response units▶
http://www.phillymag.com/news/2012/11/02/video-national-guard-rescue-jersey/

flooding▶
http://www.businessinsider.com/hurricane-sandy-photos-of-new-york-subway-flooded-2012-10

cancelled the New York Marathon▶
http://communities.washingtontimes.com/neighborhood/sports-around/2012/nov/2/bloomberg-cancels-nyc-marathon-public-outrage-sand/

Dr. Charles Stanley▶
http://en.wikipedia.org/wiki/Charles_Stanley

related▶
http://www.intouch.org/you/sermon-outlines/content?topic=our_anchor_in_times_of_storm_sermon_outline

link▶
https://www.biblegateway.com/passage/?search=1+Corinthians+10%3A1-13&version=NKJV

The Anchor Holds▶
https://www.youtube.com/watch?v=FL112E3NjqU&sns=em

Watch▶
https://www.youtube.com/watch?v=FL112E3NjqU&sns=em

The Anchor Holds▶
https://www.youtube.com/watch?v=FL112E3NjqU&sns=em

Listen and watch George Beverly Shea▶
https://www.youtube.com/watch?v=2oxRoguoTTs

In Times Like These▶
https://www.youtube.com/watch?v=2oxRoguoTTs

Our Anchor in Times of Storm▶
http://www.intouch.org/you/sermon-
outlines/content?topic=our_anchor_in_times_of_storm_sermon_outline

The Anchor Holds▶
http://www.intouch.org/you/sermon-
outlines/content?topic=our_anchor_in_times_of_storm_sermon_outline

In Times Like These▶
https://www.youtube.com/watch?v=2oxRoguoTTs

He Restoreth My Soul▶
https://www.youtube.com/watch?v=nWRoKU-r-Gk&feature=youtube_gdata

He'll Hold My Hand▶
https://www.youtube.com/watch?v=h9StneDSolQ&feature=youtube_gdata

---

..... 03

Troubled Asset Relief Program (TARP) ▶
http://en.wikipedia.org/wiki/Troubled_Asset_Relief_Program

Patient Protection and Affordable Care Act (PPACA) ▶
http://en.wikipedia.org/wiki/Troubled_Asset_Relief_Program

Tea Party movement▶
http://en.wikipedia.org/wiki/Tea_Party_movement

U.S. National Debt Clock▶
http://www.usdebtclock.org/

Islamic Republic of Iran▶
http://en.wikipedia.org/wiki/Iran

Acts 9:1-22; Acts 22:3-16; Acts 26:9-18▶ ·
https://www.biblegateway.com/passage/?search=Acts+9%3A1-22%2CActs+22%3A3-16%2CActs+26%3A9-18&version=NASB

Pharisee▶
http://en.wikipedia.org/wiki/Pharisees

persecution▶
http://en.wikipedia.org/wiki/Persecution_of_Christians_in_the_Roman_Empire

disciples▶
http://en.wikipedia.org/wiki/Disciple_%28Christianity%29

Jesus▶
http://en.wikipedia.org/wiki/Jesus

Jerusalem▶
http://en.wikipedia.org/wiki/Early_centers_of_Christianity#Jerusalem

Acts chapter 3▶
https://www.biblegateway.com/passage/?search=Acts%203&version=NASB

see Acts 2:1-13▶
https://www.biblegateway.com/passage/?search=Acts%202:1-13&version=NASB

willing to do what is right in the sight of God▶
http://jimdavenport.me/2012/10/14/calling-evil-good/

Turn your life over to Him▶
http://jimdavenport.me/2011/03/05/how-to-become-a-christian/

He Made A Change▶
https://www.youtube.com/watch?v=_2CKYLdK7XI

The Plan of Salvation▶
https://www.youtube.com/watch?v=CHWTq0SqTQQ

He Made a Change▶
https://www.youtube.com/watch?v=_2CKYLdK7XI

The Plan of Salvation▶
https://www.youtube.com/watch?v=CHWTq0SqTQQ

link▶
http://jimdavenport.me/the-good-news/

….. 04

http://www.facebook.com/video/video.php?v=488452018044 ► https://www.facebook.com/video/video.php?v=488452018044

….. 05

Jewish explanation of bloodguilt►
http://en.wikipedia.org/wiki/Ten_Commandments#cite_ref-50

abortion statistics compiled by the NRLC►
https://drive.google.com/file/d/0B_sm7pNmpvT5Q0t3MnVibERYMTg/view?pli=1

Fifty Million Lost Lives Since 1973►
https://drive.google.com/file/d/0B_sm7pNmpvT5TnF0UTZTektwazA/view?pli=1

….. 06

killing of unborn babies►
http://jimdavenport.me/2012/07/01/on-child-sacrifice/

Roe v. Wade►
http://en.wikipedia.org/wiki/Roe_v._Wade

New King James Version►
http://en.wikipedia.org/wiki/New_King_James_Version

salvation►
http://jimdavenport.me/2011/03/05/how-to-become-a-christian/

America's Future►
http://www.intouch.org/you/sermon-outlines/content?topic=america_s_future_sermon_outline

Genesis 1:27▶
https://www.biblegateway.com/passage/?search=Genesis%201:27&version=ESV

Genesis 2:16-17▶
https://www.biblegateway.com/passage/?search=Genesis+2%3A16-17&version=ESV

Genesis 3:5▶
https://www.biblegateway.com/passage/?search=Genesis%203:5&version=ESV

Exodus 20:3▶
https://www.biblegateway.com/passage/?search=Exodus%2020:3&version=ESV

branches of the United States government▶
http://en.wikipedia.org/wiki/Separation_of_powers_under_the_United_States_Constitution

deism▶
http://en.wikipedia.org/wiki/Deism

The Age of Reason▶
http://en.wikipedia.org/wiki/The_Age_of_Reason

free rational inquiry▶
http://en.wikipedia.org/wiki/The_Age_of_Reason#Intellectual_context:_eighteenth-century_British_deism

How to Become a Christian▶
http://jimdavenport.me/2011/03/05/how-to-become-a-christian/

200 murdered children▶
http://en.wikipedia.org/wiki/Jonestown

On Child Sacrifice▶
http://jimdavenport.me/2011/01/25/on-the-sanctity-of-life-and-abortion/

On the Sanctity of Life and Abortion▶
http://jimdavenport.me/2011/01/25/on-the-sanctity-of-life-and-abortion/

Lifestyle Choices and Biblical Truth▶
http://jimdavenport.me/2011/01/25/on-the-sanctity-of-life-and-abortion/

The Sanctity of Marriage▶
http://jimdavenport.me/2012/05/25/the-sanctity-of-marriage/

In His Own Image ▶
http://jimdavenport.me/2011/12/27/in-his-own-image/

Blue Letter Bible ▶
http://www.blueletterbible.org/faq/don_stewart/stewart.cfm?id=414

My Heart Aches for America ▶
http://billygraham.org/story/billy-graham-my-heart-aches-for-america/

http://jimdavenport.me/2012/04/09/when-god-has-had-enough/

Mao Tse Tung ▶
http://en.wikipedia.org/wiki/Mao_Zedong

Idi Amin ▶
http://en.wikipedia.org/wiki/Idi_Amin

Adolf Hitler ▶
http://en.wikipedia.org/wiki/Adolf_Hitler

Saddam Hussein ▶
http://en.wikipedia.org/wiki/Saddam_Hussein

Fidel Castro ▶
http://en.wikipedia.org/wiki/Fidel_Castro

Jim Jones ▶
http://en.wikipedia.org/wiki/Jim_Jones

David Koresh ▶
http://en.wikipedia.org/wiki/David_Koresh

Branch Davidian religious sect ▶
http://en.wikipedia.org/wiki/Branch_Davidians

Osama Bin Laden ▶
http://en.wikipedia.org/wiki/Osama_bin_Laden

al-Qaeda ▶
http://en.wikipedia.org/wiki/Al-Qaeda

Kim Jon Il ▶
http://en.wikipedia.org/wiki/Kim_Jong-il

….. 08

In His Time - Maranatha! Singers - Video One▶
https://www.youtube.com/watch?v=URdDVDA0WwQ&feature=youtube_gdata_p
layer

In His Time - Video Two▶
https://www.youtube.com/watch?v=8gTQvpMeh1A&feature=youtube_gdata_play
er

….. 10

Sin's Earthly Consequences▶
http://jimdavenport.me/2012/05/18/sins-earthly-consequences/

Gallup poll▶
http://www.gallup.com/poll/124793/this-christmas-78-americans-identify-
christian.aspx

Gay Marriage Rally▶
http://jimdavenport.me/2012/05/25/gay-marriage-rally/

….. 11

When God Has Had Enough▶
http://jimdavenport.me/2012/04/09/when-god-has-had-enough/

How To Become A Christian▶
http://jimdavenport.me/2011/03/05/how-to-become-a-christian/

Sin Will Take You Farther▶
https://www.youtube.com/watch?v=02Rd2_hp084&feature=youtube_gdata

….. 12

In His Time▶

http://jimdavenport.me/2012/04/24/in-his-time/

How To Become A Christian▶
http://jimdavenport.me/2011/03/05/how-to-become-a-christian/

When I Get Carried Away – The Good News▶
https://www.youtube.com/watch?v=W-rTtuW-Y9Q

….. 13

June 17, 1996 article to read more about the fire▶
https://drive.google.com/file/d/0B_sm7pNmpvT5NVFNN19KYlJtUkU/view?pli=1

article by Michael Fumento▶
https://drive.google.com/file/d/0B_sm7pNmpvT5aU9vOGo3VDVqMjA/view?pli=1

On Christians Spreading Rumors and Gossip in the Church▶
http://jimdavenport.me/2011/06/09/on-christians-spreading-rumors-and-gossip-in-the-church/

….. 14

Open Windows▶
http://www.lifeway.com/Open-Windows-Magazine/c/N-1z1407u

Marvin Minton▶
http://www.crbch.com/

How to Become a Christian▶
http://jimdavenport.me/2011/03/05/how-to-become-a-christian/

….. 15

heart biopsy▶
http://www.webmd.com/heart-disease/guide/myocardial-biopsy

heart block▶
http://en.wikipedia.org/wiki/Heart_block

atrial fibrillation▶
http://en.wikipedia.org/wiki/Atrial_fibrillation

ventricular tachycardia▶
http://en.wikipedia.org/wiki/Ventricular_tachycardia

ventricular fibrillation▶
http://en.wikipedia.org/wiki/Ventricular_fibrillation

ventricular ablation▶
http://en.wikipedia.org/wiki/Catheter_ablation

neurotransmitters▶
http://en.wikipedia.org/wiki/Neurotransmitter

Nothing is too hard for God▶
http://jimdavenport.me/2011/02/08/is-anything-too-hard-for-god/

accepted His son Jesus as my Savior and Lord▶
http://jimdavenport.me/2011/03/05/how-to-become-a-christian/

Victory Over Anxiety▶
http://www.intouch.org/you/sermon-
outlines/content?topic=victory_over_anxiety_sermon_outline
In Touch Ministries▶

trusted God's Son, Jesus Christ, as your Savior and Lord▶
http://jimdavenport.me/2011/03/05/how-to-become-a-christian/
links▶
http://jimdavenport.me/2011/03/05/how-to-become-a-christian/

───────────────────────

..... 16

───────────────────────

interview▶
http://www.bpnews.net/38271

Russian Revolution▶
http://en.wikipedia.org/wiki/Russian_Revolution

Hitler▶
http://en.wikipedia.org/wiki/Adolf_Hitler

1911▶

http://en.wikipedia.org/wiki/Xinhai_Revolution

1949▶
http://en.wikipedia.org/wiki/Chinese_Communist_Revolution

French Revolution▶
http://en.wikipedia.org/wiki/French_Revolution

Exodus 20▶
https://www.biblegateway.com/passage/?search=Exodus%2020&version=ESV

Wall Street Journal article▶
http://online.wsj.com/news/articles/SB1000142405274870462130457626711352 4583554?mg=reno64-
wsj&url=http%3A%2F%2Fonline.wsj.com%2Farticle%2FSB1000142405274870 462130457626711352 4583554.html

Baptist Press article▶
http://www.bpnews.net/38271

reported▶
http://news.blogs.cnn.com/2012/07/27/how-the-chick-fil-a-same-sex-marriage-controversy-has-evolved/

firestorm of criticism on social media▶
http://news.blogs.cnn.com/2012/07/19/chick-fil-a-and-gay-marriage-a-social-media-storm/

Scholarship Fact Sheet▶
www.truettcathy.com/pdfs/ScholarshipFactSheet.pdf

Chick-fil-A Controversy Reveals Religious Liberty Under Threat▶
http://religion.blogs.cnn.com/2012/07/31/my-take-chick-fil-a-controversy-reveals-religious-liberty-under-threat/

1 Timothy 6:6-10▶
https://www.biblegateway.com/passage/?search=1+Timothy+6%3A6-10%2C1+Timothy+6%3A17-19&version=ESV

1 Kings 3:1-15▶
https://www.biblegateway.com/passage/?search=1+Kings+3%3A1-15&version=ESV

Proverbs 11:4▶
https://www.biblegateway.com/passage/?search=Proverbs+11%3A4&version=ES V

Luke 12:13-21▶
https://www.biblegateway.com/passage/?search=Luke%2012:13-21&version=ESV

..... 17

become a Christian▶
http://jimdavenport.me/how-to-become-a-christian/

The Barna Group▶
https://www.barna.org/

devotional▶
https://docs.google.com/document/d/19_c9Vr_3Nf5TXdpdTJgGs4i4agJmI4ynt6lC
QdTGgXg/edit?pli=1

Jeremiah chapter 32▶
https://www.biblegateway.com/passage/?search=Jeremiah+32&version=NIV

Anathoth▶
http://en.wikipedia.org/wiki/Anathoth

Matthew Henry's Commentary▶
http://www.christnotes.org/commentary.php?com=mhc&b=24&c=32

nothing is too hard for Him▶
http://jimdavenport.me/2011/02/08/is-anything-too-hard-for-god/

hears ALL of our prayers▶
https://www.biblegateway.com/blog/2014/07/does-god-ever-refuse-to-answer-our-
prayers/

Psalm 66:16-20▶
https://www.biblegateway.com/passage/?search=Psalm+66%3A16-
20&version=NIV

Believing IN Christ Jesus through ALL things▶
http://believinginchristjesus.wordpress.com/

God is able to accomplish INFINITELY more than we ask▶
http://believinginchristjesus.wordpress.com/2012/06/12/god-is-able-to-accomplish-
infinitely-more-than-we-ask/

watch the video▶
https://www.youtube.com/watch?v=e9KPQTtaDoY

Ah Lord God►
https://www.youtube.com/watch?v=e9KPQTtaDoY

Is Anything Too Hard for God►
http://jimdavenport.me/2011/02/08/is-anything-too-hard-for-god/

God is able to accomplish INFINITELY more than we ask►
http://believinginchristjesus.wordpress.com/2012/06/12/god-is-able-to-accomplish-infinitely-more-than-we-ask/

Pray with Confidence►
https://docs.google.com/document/d/19_c9Vr_3Nf5TXdpdTJgGs4i4agJmI4ynt6lCQdTGgXg/edit?pli=1

Does God Ever Refuse to Hear Our Prayers►
https://www.biblegateway.com/blog/2014/07/does-god-ever-refuse-to-answer-our-prayers/

….. 18

Yiddish►
http://en.wikipedia.org/wiki/Yiddish_language

שייִיד►
http://en.wiktionary.org/wiki/%D7%99%D7%99%D6%B4%D7%93%D7%99%D7%A9

שאידי►
http://en.wiktionary.org/wiki/%D7%90%D7%99%D7%93%D7%99%D7%A9

Jewish►
http://en.wikipedia.org/wiki/Jews

High German language►
http://en.wikipedia.org/wiki/High_German_languages

Ashkenazi Jewish►
http://en.wikipedia.org/wiki/Ashkenazi_Jews

Aramaic►
http://en.wikipedia.org/wiki/Aramaic_language

Slavic►
http://en.wikipedia.org/wiki/Slavic_languages

Romance languages▶
http://en.wikipedia.org/wiki/Romance_languages

written▶
http://en.wikipedia.org/wiki/Yiddish_orthography

Hebrew alphabet▶
http://en.wikipedia.org/wiki/Hebrew_alphabet

The Plan of Salvation▶
https://www.youtube.com/watch?v=CHWTq0SqTQQ

In His Time▶
http://jimdavenport.me/2012/04/24/in-his-time/

Lifestyle Choices and Biblical Truth▶
http://jimdavenport.me/2011/11/04/lifestyle-choices-and-biblical-truth/

Seven Keys to Successful Christian Living▶
http://jimdavenport.me/2011/11/16/seven-keys-to-successful-christian-living/

"Do!" – A Call to Right Christian Action▶
http://jimdavenport.me/2011/11/23/do/

The Believer's Sufficiency in Christ▶
http://jimdavenport.me/2011/11/30/the-believers-sufficiency-in-christ/

In His Own Image▶
http://jimdavenport.me/2011/12/27/in-his-own-image/

How to Become a Christian▶
http://jimdavenport.me/2011/03/05/how-to-become-a-christian/

The Plan of Salvation▶
https://www.youtube.com/watch?v=CHWTq0SqTQQ

Listen to The Good News▶
http://jimdavenport.me/the-good-news/

….. 19

An Attitude of Thankfulness▶
http://jimdavenport.me/2012/11/13/an-attitude-of-thankfulness/

1 Chronicles 5►
https://www.biblegateway.com/passage/?search=1%20Chronicles%205&version=ESV

A Roman Coin minted in 56 AD Depicting Nero►
http://www.ancientcoins.ca/RIC/RIC1/RIC1_Nero_1-200.htm

2 Corinthians 13:1►
https://www.biblegateway.com/passage/?search=2%20Corinthians%2013:1&version=ESV

Acts 20:2►
https://www.biblegateway.com/passage/?search=Acts+20%3A2&version=ESV

America Under Judgement►
http://billygraham.org/decision-magazine/november-2012/america-under-judgment/

..... 20

----

listen now►
https://www.youtube.com/watch?v=QujktHJWCj8

In His Time►
http://jimdavenport.me/?s=in+his+time

Become A Christian►
http://jimdavenport.me/how-to-become-a-christian/

God Will Provide►
https://www.youtube.com/watch?v=QujktHJWCj8

http://www.familylife.com►
http://www.familylife.com/

Day 3 of God Has Not Forgotten You►
http://www.familylife.com/articles/topics/faith/essentials/growing-in-your-faith/god-has-not-forgotten-you-a-31-day-devotional#.UP3TL_Jv6So

When Trouble Knocks►
http://www.cbn.com/spirituallife/devotions/irvin_trouble.aspx

God Has Not Forgotten You►

http://www.familylife.com/articles/topics/faith/essentials/growing-in-your-faith/god-has-not-forgotten-you-a-31-day-devotional#.UP3TL_Jv6So

---

….. How to Become a Christian

More help on How to Become a Christian▶
http://www.sbc.net/knowjesus/theplan.asp

Books by Jim Davenport

Christian Devotions and Quick Studies
Thanksgiving Day – Religious to Secular
The Fall of a Godly Nation
An Attitude of Thankfulness
Thank You Lord for Saving My Soul

Preview and Order Books by Jim Davenport
http://jimdavenport.me/jims-books/

Jim's books are available for all of the popular eReaders such as the Kindle, Apple iPad/iBooks, Nook, Sony Reader, Kobo, Palm, Web Browser, RTF (viewable with most word processors), PDF, and most PC based e-reading apps including Stanza, Aldiko, and Adobe Digital Editions, among others.

Not everyone wants to go to the internet to read Christian articles and not everyone has a computer … thus I also have printed books available. You can support Jim's writing ministry by purchasing one of his books at this link:

Preview and Order Books by Jim Davenport
http://jimdavenport.me/jims-books/

For additional information address:

Jim Davenport
InfoSys Solutions Associates, Inc.
6637 Burnt Hickory Drive
Hoschton, GA 30548

jimdavenport.me
jamesldavenport@gmail.com